Simeon Thayer

The Invasion of Canada in 1775

Simeon Thayer

The Invasion of Canada in 1775

ISBN/EAN: 9783743332430

Manufactured in Europe, USA, Canada, Australia, Japa

Cover: Foto ©ninafisch / pixelio.de

Manufactured and distributed by brebook publishing software
(www.brebook.com)

Simeon Thayer

The Invasion of Canada in 1775

THE INVASION OF CANADA IN 1775:

INCLUDING THE

Journal of Captain Simeon Thayer,

DESCRIBING THE

PERILS AND SUFFERINGS

OF THE

ARMY UNDER COLONEL BENEDICT ARNOLD,

IN ITS MARCH

THROUGH THE WILDERNESS TO QUEBEC:

With Notes and Appendix.

BY EDWIN MARTIN STONE.

PROVIDENCE:
KNOWLES, ANTHONY & CO., PRINTERS.
1867.

PREFACE.

THE JOURNAL of Captain SIMEON THAYER makes no pretension to literary merit. It was written, doubtless, to keep fresh in the memory of the author the facts of his personal experience during his march through the wilderness to Quebec, as well as of his confinement while prisoner of war, without expectation of its ever appearing in print. It is here reproduced as it stands in the original, without any change of capital letters or of orthography, and with only such added punctuation as was thought necessary to render clear the meaning of the text. For this reason a number of words will be found incorrectly spelled. The Introduction, Notes and Appendix, are the results of extensive research. The first is prefixed, and the latter are added, to give completeness to the story of one of the most daring and important military enterprises of the Revolutionary War. A Bibliography of the Journals published on the subject, so far as is known, and also a list of works which treat more or less fully upon the Invasion of Canada, is herewith annexed — the first that has ever been attempted—for the convenience of students of this portion of American history. Possibly some Journals of "Arnold's Expedition" have been published that have escaped attention, and it is by no means certain that the list of reference works is complete. Additions under either of these heads are earnestly solicited, and will be gratefully acknowledged. For facts and documents communicated to the editor of the Journal, special thanks are tendered to Samuel G. Drake, Esq., of Boston; Rev. Richard Eddy, Librarian Pennsylvania Historical Society; Hon. M. H. Taggart, State Treasurer, Pennsylvania; Henry T. Drowne, Esq., New York; George H. Moore, Esq., Librarian New York Historical Society; Richard R. Ward, Esq., Brooklyn, N. Y.; Charles J. Hoadly, Esq., Secretary Connecticut Historical Society; John G. Metcalf, M. D., Mendon, Mass.; Simon Henry Greene, Esq., River Point, R. I.; David King, M. D., Newport, R. I.; William W. Burr, Stephen T. Olney, and Crawford Allen, Esqs., Providence, R. I.

E. M. S.

Providence, R. I., January 19, 1867.

WORKS RELATING TO THE INVASION OF CANADA.

ARNOLD'S JOURNAL. Colonel Benedict Arnold kept a Journal of his expedition. It was left by him at West Point, when he fled on hearing of the capture of Andre, and was found among his papers by Judge Pierpont Edwards, of Connecticut, who was appointed to administer upon the goods and estate of Arnold, his treason making him dead in law. The Manuscript was in existence in 1835, though in rather a dilapidated state. The writing was in the middle style between copy and running hand. Extracts from this Journal were published in the appendix to the Life of Burr, by Samuel L. Knapp, 1835, beginning Sept. 27, and ending Oct. 30, 1775. They confirm the accuracy of the statements in Capt. Thayer's Journal, but throw no additional light upon the history of the expedition.

MCCOY'S JOURNAL. Judge Henry states that Sergeant William McCoy, of Captain Hendricks' company, while in confinement in Quebec, gave to Major Murphy, of the British Garrison, a correct copy of a Journal kept by himself through the wilderness. Whether it was carried to England, is not known. It probably was never published. Possibly it may be in existence.

FRENCH JOURNALS. John G. Shea, Esq., of New York, brought from Canada two Journals in Manuscript, written respectively by French Notaries; one at Quebec, and the other at Three Rivers, "about *the Invasion of the Bostonnais*." The word *Bostonnais* was a designation intended to apply to nearly all New England. The word was found by George Gibbs in the Chinook Jargon in Oregon, and he could not account for it. The titles of the two French Journals, however, explain it. In Indian, *Wastonrouon;* W being substituted for the B amongst the Indians.

AN ACCURATE AND INTERESTING ACCOUNT of the hardships and sufferings of that Band of Heroes, who traversed the Wilderness in the Campaign against Quebec, in 1775. By John Joseph Henry, Esq. Late President of the Second Judicial District of Pennsylvania. Lancaster: Printed by William Greer, 1812. pp. 225, small 12mo.

THE SAME—LIBRARY EDITION. Campaign against Quebec, | being | an accurate and interesting account | of the | Hardships and Sufferings | of that | BAND OF HEROES | who traversed the Wilderness | by the route of the Kennebec and Chaudiere Rivers | to Quebec, in the year 1775. | By John Joseph Henry, Esq. | Late President of the second Judicial District in Pennsylvania. | Revised edition, with corrections and alterations. | Watertown, N. Y. | Printed and Published by Knowlton & Rice, | 1844. | pp. 212, 16mo. [Sketch of the Life of Arnold copied mainly from Sparks' Biography, at the end of the second edition in place of notes in the first edition.]

HETH'S JOURNAL. Lieutenant [afterwards Colonel] William Heth, 2d, kept a Journal of Arnold's Expedition, which is referred to in Marshall's Life of Washington, Vol. I., pp. 53, 67, second edition. It is thought to have been published in Virginia.

A JOURNAL of the hardships and privations endured by the troops in this expedition was kept by Caleb Haskell, of Newburyport, Mass., a private in Capt. Ward's company, but was never published.

LETTERS of Colonel, generally known as Major Henry Caldwell, written on board the Hunter, British armed vessel, relate particularly to the attack on Quebec.

A JOURNAL OF THE EXPEDITION TO QUEBEC, in the year 1775, under the command of Colonel Benedict Arnold. By James Melvin, a private in Captain Dearborn's company. New York: 1857. With Introductory Remarks and Notes by W. J. D. Large 8vo, tinted paper: pp. 30. 100 copies only printed.

This Journal commences at Cambridge, Sept. 13, 1775, and terminates at Quebec, Aug. 5, 1776. It was edited by William J. Davis, Esq., late private Secretary of Hon. George Bancroft. Of the author nothing is known beyond the statement made in the title page. W. J. D. says, "The style of the composition, and exceedingly neat penmanship of the Journal, is strong evidence, however, that he possessed, for the times, considerable education." The Journal, as a contribution to the history of Arnold's Expedition, is of great value.

THE SAME, with Introduction and copious Notes, printed for the Franklin Club, Philadelphia, 1864. 100 copies 8vo.; 20 quarto.

JOURNAL OF THE EXPEDITION AGAINST QUEBEC, under command of Colonel Benedict Arnold, in the year 1775, by Major Return J. Meigs, with Introduction and Notes by Charles J. Bushnell. New York: Privately printed, 1864. 8vo. fine tinted paper, with portrait of Colonel Christopher Greene. pp. 57.

This Journal begins Sept. 9, at Roxbury, and closes at Quebec, January 1, 1776. The Notes are full and valuable. The Journal was printed in the Massachusetts Historical Collections, Second Series, Vol. II.

MANUSCRIPTS RELATING TO THE EARLY HISTORY OF CANADA. Published under the auspices of the Literary and Historical Society of Quebec. Quebec: Printed by Middleton and Davis, Shaw's Building, 1866.

THE JOURNAL OF ISAAC SENTER, Physician and Surgeon to the troops detached from the American Army encamped at Cambridge, Mass., on a Secret Expedition against Quebec, under the command of Colonel Benedict Arnold, in September, 1775. Philadelphia: Published by the Historical Society of Pennsylvania, 1846. To this edition is prefixed a brief notice of the Manuscript of the Journal, and a biographical preface. A few notes of reference are added.

This Journal was carried to Philadelphia, where it was lost sight of for many years, and finally came into the hands of Dr. Lewis Roper, of that city, whose perception of its importance induced him to communicate it to the Pennsylvania Historical Society. It commences at Cambridge, September 13th, 1775, and closes at Quebec, January 6, 1776. The position of Dr. Senter in the Expedition imparts to it a special value.

JOURNAL OF CAPTAIN SIMEON THAYER, describing the perils and sufferings endured by Arnold's detachment in their march through the Wilderness of Maine and Canada to Quebec in 1775. Now first printed.

CAPTAIN JOHN TOPHAM'S JOURNAL of the Expedition to Quebec, through the Wilderness of Maine, in September, October and November, 1775. Not published.

The first part of this Journal has been unfortunately lost by being worn off by use and careless handling. It commences sometime before the 20th September, but in its present dilapidated state, the legible part begins October 6, 1775. The last part is gone, and the manuscript ends at a time while Captain Topham was still a prisoner at Quebec. The Journal is in the possession of David King, M. D., of Newport, R. I.

A JOURNAL OF A MARCH FROM CAMBRIDGE on an Expedition against Quebec, in Col. Benedict Arnold's Detachment, Sept. 13, 1775. Kept by Joseph Ware, of Needham, Mass. Published in the New England Historical and Genealogical Register, Vol. VI., 1852, with Notes by Justin Winsor, of Boston.

The author was a private in Captain Samuel Ward's company. The Journal is one of the most valuable that have been printed.

Arnold's History of Rhode Island, Vol. II.
Allen's Biographical Dictionary.
Annual Register, London, 1776.
Amwell's History.
American Archives, 5th Series.
Bosworth's History of Montreal

Bancroft's History of the United States, Vol. VIII.
Botta's American Revolution.
Bloodgood's Sexagenary, or Reminiscences of the Revolution, 1866.
Colonial Records of Rhode Island.
Correspondence of the American Revolution, Vol. I.
Connecticut State Papers—War.
Dunlap's History of New York, Vol. II.
Davis's Memoirs of Aaron Burr, Vol. I.
Gordon's American Revolution, Vols. I and II.
Hawkins' Picture of Quebec.
Holt's Paper, New York.
Historical and Genealogical Register, Boston.
Knapp's Life of Aaron Burr.
Life of Ethan Allen, or "Allen's Narrative."
Life of Richard Montgomery.
Life of Benedict Arnold.
Life of General Daniel Morgan.
Life and Correspondence of Joseph Reed.
Life and Times of Gen. John Lamb, by Isaac Q. Leake.
Lossing's Field Book of the Revolution, Vol. I.
Maine Historical Society's Collections, Vol. I.
Massachusetts Historical Society's Collections, 2d Series.
Madame De Reidesel's Journal.
Marshall's Life of Washington.
Parton's Life of Aaron Burr.
Peterson's History of Rhode Island.
Providence Gazette and Country Journal, 1776.
Palmer's History of Lake Champlain.
Remembrancer.
Rogers' Biographical Dictionary.
Silliman's tour between Hartford and Quebec, 1819.
Trumbull's Reminiscences of his own Times.
Thatcher's Military Journal.
Writings of Washington, Vol. III.
Wilkinson's Memoirs, Vol. I.
Warren's History of the American Revolution.

ADDENDA TO WORKS ON THE INVASION OF CANADA,

DEARBORN'S JOURNAL. It is understood that Captain Henry Dearborn kept a Journ of his march through the wilderness, and of his experiences while a prisoner at Quebec but it is not known to have been printed.

HISTORY OF CANADA, by Andrew Bell, 2 vols.

HOLLISTER'S History of Connecticut.

IRVING'S Life of Washington contains several chapters relating to the Invasion of Canada, and some references.

JOURNALS OF CONGRESS. The Journals of the Proceedings of the Continental Congress, in 1776, contain interesting facts relating to the Invasion of Canada. The volumes for 1775 and 1776 should not be overlooked by the historical student.

JOURNAL of Madame De Reidesel, translated by William L. Stone. This new translation gives the portions of the Journal hitherto suppressed, touching American Slavery.

JOURNAL, (MS.) kept at Three Rivers in 1775—6, by M. Badeux, a Royalist Notary.

JOURNAL kept during the seige of Fort St. John, by one of its defenders, (M. Antoine Foucher.)

JOURNAL, (MS.) of Sanguinet, a Montreal Barrister.

Two of the above Journals have already been referred to p. iv, under the head of "French Journals."

MEMOIRES DE SANGUINET. (MS.)

MORGAN'S Sketches of celebrated Canadians.

PEIRCE'S JOURNAL. Of this Journal and its author, Charles Congdon, Esq., Treasurer of the Bradford Club,* in New York, has kindly communicated the following particulars: It is a closely written manuscript, containing the daily occurrences from September 8th, 1775, to January 16th, 1776. The first leaf, and several leaves at the end, are unfortunately wanting. The author, John Peirce, was of Worcester, Mass. He belonged to the contingent, and as Engineer and Surveyor was attached to one of the parties mentioned by Meigs and Henry as being sent forward from Fort Western to establish the bearings of the route through the wilderness. This Journal, it is believed, has not hitherto been known to any of our historians.

SEDGWICK'S History of Sharon.

STATEMENT OF THE EXPEDITION TO CANADA, &c. By Lieut. Gen. Burgoyne. Six maps. Quarto, untrimmed, boards, 1780. Octavo, bound, second edition, 1780.

ACKNOWLEDGMENTS. In the acknowledgments of courtesies, the names of A. W. Green, Esq., Librarian of the New York Mercantile Library Association, and of Francis Lawton, Esq., Newport, R. I., should have been included.

ERRATA. Preface. The residence of Richard R. Ward, Esq., is New York. The middle initial in Mr. Bushnell's name should be I.

---

*The publications of the BRADFORD CLUB have reached six in number, the first being "Hatfield and Deerfield," and all in the highest style of art. One hundred copies only of Melvin's Journal were printed for the Club.

INTRODUCTION.

INVASION OF CANADA.

WHEN, early in 1775, a breach with the Mother Country seemed inevitable, and far-sighted men like the Adamses, Samuel Ward and Patrick Henry, perceived in the events of the hour the embryo of an Independent Nation, the leaders of popular rights cast about for help to strengthen their plans when they should be developed in positive action. They naturally looked to Canada as an important northern barrier. The interests of the French population were thought to be identical with those of the Colonies, and there was reason for the belief that in a general uprising their support would readily be given. Should Canada be invaded by a provincial army, and St. John's, Montreal and Quebec secured by conquest, nothing would be in the way of the people there throwing off the British yoke.

With some, however, the invasion of Canada was not a favorite scheme. They had not gone so far yet as to decide affirmatively upon the question of National Independence, and when the first Congress met, many were decided on a further attempt to reconcile the existing difficulties, by a petition to the King.

Whatever might have been the contingent purpose of Congress in reference to Canada, a disclaimer of an intended invasion was deemed, under the circumstances, expedient; and accordingly on the 1st of June, such a disclaimer was made. But a violent proclamation issued by the British Governor, denouncing the border inhabitants of the Colonies as traitors, and inciting the Indians against New York and New England, changed the current of opinion in the Congress, and led to the avowal of an aggressive purpose. In July, preliminary to a movement of this character, Major John Brown, accompanied by four men, visited Canada for the purpose of obtaining intelligence in regard to the military preparations making there by the King's troops, the situation of St. John's, Chambly, Montreal and Quebec, and also to ascertain the feelings of the Canadians towards the Colonial cause. They found them favorably affected, were kindly received by the French, were often protected when exposed to danger, and were assured it was their wish to see a Continental army in Canada; engaging, if it came, to supply it with everything in their power. The Indians also expressed a determination to act with the Canadians. At this time there were but about seven hundred of the King's troops in Canada, of which near three hundred were at St. John's and only about fifty at Quebec. The residue were at Montreal, Chambly, and at the upper posts. Everything seemed favorable for the contemplated invasion. Major Brown and his party remained in Canada but three days, and after several hair-breadth escapes reached Crown Point August 10th, in safety.

Events had now ripened for action. Colonel Ethan Allen had taken possession of Ticonderoga, "In the name of the Great Jehovah and the Continental Congress." Crown Point had surrendered to the Provincial forces, two British vessels had been taken, which gave to the Americans the control of Lake Champlain, and thus "the gates of Canada were thrown open," inviting an unresisting entrance. Nothing now remained but to improve the opportunity by pushing forward. For this work of invasion, Generals Schuyler and Montgomery were designated, who at once began an advance from Ticonderoga. On reaching Isle-aux-Noix, Colonel Allen was sent forward with Major Brown, accompanied by interpreters, into Canada, with letters to the Canadians, to let them know that the design of the army was only against the English garrisons, and not the country, their liberties, or their religion. This undertaking, though attended with much danger, was successfully accomplished. But before the army was ready to leave the Isle-aux-Noix, General Schuyler was taken sick and returned to Albany, leaving the command with General Montgomery. He subsequently returned, with the hope of being able to move with the army, but his disorder (a bilious fever) reäppearing with increased violence, he was obliged, reluctantly, to withdraw from personal participation in the enterprise. General Schuyler had entered heartily into the scheme of getting possession of Canada, and securing it to the cause of National Freedom, and felt deeply chagrined in not being able to lead his troops forward. Writing to Washington on the subject, he says:

"The vexation of spirit under which I labor, that a barbarous complication of disorders should prevent me from reaping those laurels for which I have unweariedly wrought, since I was honored with this command; the anxiety I have suffered since my arrival here, lest the army should starve, occasioned by a scandalous want of subordination and inattention to my orders, in some of the officers I left to command at the different posts; the vast variety of disagreeable and vexatious incidents, that almost every hour arise in some department or other,—not only retard my cure, but have put me considerably back for some days past. If Job had been a General in my situation, his memory had not been so famous for patience. But the glorious end we have in view, and which I have confident hope will be attained, will atone for all."*

The army at Isle-aux-Noix, on the 10th of September, consisted of 1394 rank and file. These were reënforced by Colonel Livingston's company of New Yorkers, 170 Green Mountain Boys under Colonel Seth Warner, Captain Allen's company of the same corps raised in Connecticut, about 100 men of Colonel Bedel's from New Hampshire, and a company of artillery under Captain Lamb; the whole probably not exceeding 1800 men. Up to September 29th, 726 men were found to be unfit for further service during this campaign, and were discharged.

On the 5th of September, the army embarked at the Isle-aux-Noix for St. John's, which was at once besieged, and on the 3d of November was taken possession of by the victorious Continentals. On the 13th of the same month Montreal surrendered. Quebec† was the next object of possession, for without that the subjugation

*Gen. Schuyler's letter to Washington.

†Quebec was founded on the 3d of July, 1608, by Captain Samuel de Champlain, Geographer to the French King. His commencement was on Cape Diamond, on the site of an Indian village called Stadacone. Champlain died in Quebec, and according to tradition was buried in the upper town. This, it appears, was a mistake. Recently, the original grave was discovered in the lower town, there having been one or two removals. About ten years ago the bones were placed in a box, but where deposited is not at this time (Dec., 1866,) known.

or deliverance of Canada was impossible. To aid the invading army under Montgomery in the attempt upon that city, a coöperative expedition by the way of the Kennebec river through the wilderness of Maine and Canada, to form a junction before Quebec, was devised, and the command given to Colonel Benedict Arnold. He was well adapted to such an undertaking. He was a brave, skillful and energetic officer; was inured to the hardships of military life; was sufficiently ambitious to insure vigorous activity to all his movements, and having previous to the war, visited Quebec as a trader, he had formed an acquaintance with many of its citizens, and acquired a knowledge of its localities that could be turned to advantage in his military operations.

The following were officers in this expedition:

Colonel. Benedict Arnold,* Norwich, Conn.

Lieut. Colonels. Christopher Greene, Warwick, R. I.; Roger Enos, Conn.

Majors. Return J. Meigs, Middletown, Conn.; Timothy Bigelow, Worcester, Mass.

Lieutenant and Adjutant. Christian Febiger, Copenhagen, Denmark. *Quartermaster.* —— Hyde, Mass. *Chaplain.* Rev. Samuel Spring, Newburyport, Mass. *Surgeon.* Isaac Senter, Newport, R. I. *Surgeon's Mate.* —— Greene.

Captains. Simeon Thayer, Providence, R. I.; Samuel Ward, Westerly, R. I.; John Topham, Newport, R. I.; William Goodrich, Great Barrington, Mass.; Jonas Hubbard, Worcester, Mass.; —— Williams, Mass.; —— Scott, Mass.; Oliver Hanchet, Suffield, Conn.; Eleazer Oswald, New Haven, Conn.; William Hendricks, Penn.; Matthew Smith, Lancaster, Penn.; Henry Dearborn, East Nottingham, N. H.; Daniel Morgan, Frederick Co., Va.; —— McCobb, Georgetown. *Brigade Major.* Matthias Ogden, and Aaron Burr, volunteer, N. J.

Lieutenants. Archibald Steele, (Adjutant) Lancaster, Penn.; Michael [George?] Simpson, Penn.; Francis Nichols, Cumberland Co., Penn.; Andrew Moody; John Humphreys, Va.; William Heth, 2d, Frederick Co. Va.; Peter O'Brien Bruen, Frederick Co., Va.; Samuel Cooper, Conn.; Abijah Savage, (Quartermaster) Middletown, Conn.; Joseph Webb, Newport, R. I.; Edward Slocum, Tiverton, R. I.; William Humphrey, Providence, R. I.; Lemuel Bailey, Providence, R. I.; Sylvanus Shaw, Newport, R. I.; John Compston, Saco, (Dist. Maine) Mass.; John Clark, Hadley, Mass.; Samuel Brown, Acton, Mass.; James Tisdale, Medfield, Mass.; —— Cumstock, Mass.; Ammi [Amos?] Andrews, Hillsborough, N. H.; Nathaniel Hutchins, Dunbarton, N. H., afterwards Captain; Joseph Thomas, Deerfield, N. H., fell in the action at Quebec; —— McCleland, Penn., died in the wilderness; —— Church; Benjamin Catlin, (Quartermaster) Weathersfield, Conn.†

It will be seen by the foregoing list that Rhode Island was ably represented in this Expedition. Lieutenant Colonel Greene proved, both in the wilderness and before Quebec, that the judgment which selected him for that trying and perilous service had not been mistaken. He subsequently served with distinction as a Colonel in the Continental line, and at Red Bank crowned his name with imperishable

---

*Colonel Benedict Arnold was born in Norwich, Conn., January 3d, 1741, and consequently was thirty-four years of age when he entered upon this command. He was an able and intrepid officer, but unfortunately the victim of a low moral sense. His career as a General in the Continental army is too familiar to require particular notice. A life brilliant in promise, closed in ignominy. He died in London, June 14th, 1801, aged 60 years. See Life of Arnold in Spark's Biography.

†This list has been collected from various authentic sources. It is probably incomplete.

honor. Captain Topham was esteemed a valuable officer, and succeeded Colonel Barton in the command of a Rhode Island regiment. Captain Ward showed great energy of character and undoubted patriotism. He was promoted to be Major, and at Red Bank, and afterwards to the close of the war, met promptly and satisfactorily, the demands made upon his military abilities. Captain Thayer, who was honored after his release from imprisonment, with the rank of Major, is identified with one of the most brilliant battles of the Revolutionary war. Dr. Senter, who served so usefully in this Expedition, took position after leaving the army, as a leading physician and surgeon in the State. The under officers and privates composing Arnold's command were for the most part taken from among the yeomanry, and were men who comprehended the nature of the conflict to which they were committed. To them, the freedom of their country was dear, and to secure it they were ready to lay upon the altar their cherished personal comforts, and to abide the results of battle. Such men were likely to make good soldiers, and by their correct deportment to gain the commendation of general officers under whom they might be called to serve. And thus it proved with them. The eye of General Montgomery was quick to recognize their soldierly qualities. "I find," he said, "Colonel Arnold's corps an exceedingly fine one, inured to fatigue, and well accustomed to cannon shot (at Cambridge). There is a style of discipline among them much superior to what I have been used to see this campaign. He himself is active, intelligent and enterprising."

General Washington had carefully studied the plan for acquiring possession of Canada and inducing the native population to join their fortunes with the Americans, in rising to the dignity of a Nationality. He had a keen perception of the importance of this movement, and was solicitous that nothing should occur to mar its success. He foresaw the possibility of the invading army indulging in pillage on their march, or of committing other acts when established in the country that might convert friends into foes. To guard against this, he drew up a series of instructions, clear and explicit in their details, which were communicated to Colonel Arnold for the government of himself and his men. He was to exercise the utmost vigilance in guarding against surprisals. On arriving in Canada, he was to ascertain by every means in his power, the real sentiments of the inhabitants towards the American cause, and to maintain the strictest discipline and good order among his own troops. He was to conciliate the affections both of the Canadians and of the Indians, and convince them that his army came among them as friends and "not as robbers." He was to pay the full value for all provisions and accommodations received, and abstain from pressing the people or any of their cattle into his service, while he was "amply to compensate" those who voluntarily assisted him. Only the "King's stores" were to be appropriated to the Continental use. In case of a union with General Schuyler, who it was then expected would lead the invasion by way of St. John's and Montreal, Arnold was to serve under him, and not to consider himself "as upon a separate and independent command." He was to keep Washington acquainted with his progress and prospects, and to send the intelligence of any important occurrence by express. He was to protect and support the free exercise of the religion of the country, and the undisturbed enjoyment of the rights of conscience in religious matters. If Lord Chatham's son should be in Canada, and in any way should fall into his power, he was to treat him with all possible deference and respect. "You cannot err," said the instructions, "in paying too much honor to the son of so illustrious a character, and so true a friend to America. Any other persons who may fall into your hands, you will treat with as much humanity and kindness as may be consistent with your own safety and the public interest."

The plan of reaching Quebec by the Kennebec and Chaudiere rivers is said to have been original with Arnold, and to have been suggested to him by the perusal of a Journal of an exploring expedition from Quebec into the interior of Maine, about the year 1760, written by Colonel Montreser, an officer of Engineers in the British service.

The troops to accompany Colonel Arnold assembled at Cambridge, and on the 13th of September commenced their march to Newburyport. Previous to leaving, General Washington, with increasing solicitude for the prosperity of the Expedition, addressed a letter to Colonel Arnold, again charging him, his officers and soldiers, to respect the persons, private property and religion of the people whose country they were soon to occupy, and to refrain from every act that might militate against personal honor or the success of the enterprise. An address to the inhabitants of Canada was also printed and forwarded to Arnold at Fort Western, to be distributed among the people on his arrival at Quebec, explaining the object of the invasion, assuring them of protection, inviting them to furnish supplies for the Provincial army, and urging them to make common cause in the overthrow of tyranny by joining "the standard of general liberty."

Arnold's force consisted of thirteen companies, comprising 1100 men. These were divided into two battalions, the first commanded by Lieutenant Colonel Christopher Greene, and the second by Lieutenant Colonel Roger Enos. On the 19th of September they sailed in ten transports from Newburyport, the fleet being under the command of Captain Clarkson, and reached the Kennebec river the next day. On the 23d they arrived at Fort Western, where they remained a day or two, and then proceeded to Fort Halifax. From thence they advanced to Norridgewock, at which place they halted until the morning of October 9th, when a general movement commenced.

The army set off in high spirits. A month, however, sufficed to cool the ardor of the less sanguine. Unthought of obstacles impeded their progress. The streams were rapid and hard to navigate; boats were dashed in pieces, and the hardy voyagers barely escaped watery graves; the autumn storms were cold and piercing; encampments were flooded by overflowing rivers; swamps and morasses spread in the track of the advancing columns; little confidence was felt in the intelligence of guides who were leading them daily deeper into an almost unknown wilderness; provisions had become exhausted; roots, dog-meat, soup made of raw-hide moccasins, and entrails broiled on the coals, became luxuries; and death by starvation stared them in the face. It required nerves of steel to survey the prospect before them with calmness, much more with hope, and the question of return was often discussed. In the then crude state of military authority, the control held by officers over their men was more the result of personal regard than of deference to position. Every man had an opinion, and was free to express it. Among a portion of the troops the views of both officers and men coincided. Disaffection had extended to three companies, and it became advisable to hold a council of war for decisive measures. This took place October 25th, on reaching Dead River.

Arnold, who was ignorant of the design afterwards put in execution, had gone on with the advance. At the council, Lieutenants Colonel Greene and Enos, Major Bigelow, Captains Topham, Thayer, Ward, Williams, McCobb, Scott, Adjutant Hyde and Lieutenant Peters were present. Major Meigs, Captains Morgan, Smith, Hanchet, Hubbard, Goodrich, Hendricks and Dearborn were absent on duty. It was now a moment of anxious interest. The decision of the hour would strengthen a patriotic resolve, or fill the country with painful disappointment. In accordance with military custom the opinions of the younger officers were first elicited. Captain Ward, a youth of only eighteen years, was now called upon for his opinion. He expressed it frankly and decidedly. The idea of giving up the expedition was totally repugnant to his brave nature, and with a patriotism for which he was ever after distinguished, he gave his voice for advancing. There was power in that decision, and one can readily imagine with what a look of approval it was recognized by the gallant Greene. Captains Thayer and Topham took the same side with no less promptness, as did Lieutenants Colonel Greene and Enos, and Major Bigelow. Captains Williams, McCobb and Scott, Adjutant Hyde and Lieutenant Peters, took an opposite view. They considered the success of the Expedition hopeless, and gave their voices for returning. The decision to advance was carried by a single vote; but the minority, immediately after the dissolution of the council, conferred together, and unanimously resolved to go back with their men. As the three disaffected companies belonged to Lieutenant Colonel Enos' battalion, he decided, though as he said, reluctantly, and for reasons that he considered a justification of the step, to go back with them. This he accordingly did.*

The withdrawal of so many men was a serious loss to Arnold, but did not in the least shake his determination to see Quebec. To facilitate the advance of the army, he had sent forward a party consisting of Lieutenant Archibald Steele, Jesse Wheeler, John Joseph Henry, George Merchant, James Clifton, Robert Cunningham, Thomas Boyd, John Tidd, John McKonkey, Jeremiah Getchel and John Horne, the two latter being guides, for the purpose of finding and marking the paths used by the Indians at the numerous carrying places in the wilderness, and also to ascertain the course of the Chaudiere river. Provided with two birch bark canoes, they set out in high spirits, and travelled until October 8th, blazing trees and "snagging bushes" with their tomahawks, when they reached the height of land which divides the waters of New England from those of Canada. Another day brought them to the Chaudiere river, when they commenced their return. They continued their course until October 17th, when, to their great joy, they fell in with a party of pioneers building a causeway for the passage of the army, having suffered excessively from hunger and exhaustion.

Sickness, the concomitant of exposure, soon made its appearance among the troops. On the seventh day after leaving Norridgewock, fatigue, diarrhœa and rheumatism had so multiplied the sick, as to render the erection of a building for their reception necessary. Accordingly a block house was built and named "Arnold's Hospital," which was immediately filled. Among the patients was a young gentleman by the name of Irvin, an Ensign in Captain Morgan's company. He was a native of Pennsylvania, and had been educated for the medical profession. Early in the march from Cambridge, he was seized with dysentery, for which he could not be prevailed upon to take medicine. Wading in the water by day, and sleeping on the ground at night, brought on a violent rheumatism, which swelled the joints of his extremities to an enormous size, and rendered them inflexible. He was left at the hospital to be sent back with others.*

Weakened as the little army was by the defection of three companies, the courage and spirit of the remaining ten still held good. Scouting the idea of abandoning the Expedition, they continued their advance to the Chaudiere river, and thence to Sartigan, a Canadian settlement, where they arrived November 3d. Here, the next day, Colonel Arnold was waited upon by a body of savages accompanied by an interpreter, to inquire his reason for coming among them in a hostile manner. They addressed him in great pomp, and one of their chiefs delivered an oration with all the air and gesture of an accomplished orator. After this being explained or translated, the Colonel returned the following answer:

"FRIENDS AND BRETHREN:—I feel myself very happy in meeting with so many of my brethren from the different quarters of the great country, and more so as I find we meet as friends, and that we are equally concerned in this expedition. Brethren, we are the chil-

*See Journal, pp. 10, 11.

dren of those people who have now taken up the hatchet against us. More than one hundred years ago, we were all as one family. We then differed in our religion, and came over to this great country by consent of the King. Our fathers bought land of the savages, and have grown a great people. Even as the stars in the sky. We have planted the ground, and by our labor grow rich. Now a new King and his wicked great men want to take our lands and money without our consent. This we think unjust, and all our great men from the river St. Lawrence to the Mississippi, met together at Philadelphia, where they all talked together, and sent a prayer to the King, that they would be brothers and fight for him, but would not give up their lands and money. The King would not hear our prayer, but sent a great army to Boston, and endeavored to set our brethren against us in Canada. The King's army at Boston came out into the fields and houses, killed a great many women and children, while they were peaceably at work. The Bostonians sent to their brethren in the country, and they came in unto their relief, and in six days raised an army of fifty thousand men, and drove the King's troops on board their ships, killed and wounded fifteen hundred of their men. Since that they durst not come out of Boston. Now we hear the French and Indians in Canada have sent to us, that the King's troops oppress them and make them pay a great price for their rum, &c.; press them to take up arms against the Bostonians, their brethren, who have done them no hurt. By the desire of the French and Indians, our brothers, we have come to their assistance, with an intent to drive out the King's soldiers; when drove off we will return to our country, and leave this to the peaceable enjoyment of its proper inhabitants. Now if the Indians, our brethren, will join us, we will be very much obliged to them, and will give them one Portuguese per month, two dollars bounty, and find them their provisions, and they liberty to choose their own officers."

This declaration had the desired effect. About fifty of them embodied according to agreement, took their canoes and proceeded.*

Soon after the battle of Bunker Hill, Aaron Burr, accompanied by his friend Matthias Ogden, set out from Elizabethtown, N. J., for Cambridge, to offer his services to the Colonial cause. Burr had now entered his twentieth year, and with an enthusiastic and adventurous nature, he gladly improved the opportunity to join Arnold, as a volunteer, in this expedition. The step was contrary to the wishes of his friends, one of whom followed him to Newburyport to induce him to return. Entreaties proving unavailing, he was furnished with a small sum of gold to meet necessary incidental expenses. He continued with Arnold, sharing in the privations of his companions until the army reached Chandiere Pond, when he was despatched with a verbal message to General Montgomery. Disguised as a young Catholic Priest, he proceeded on his journey, which was successfully accomplished. Pleased with the appearance of Burr, General Montgomery at once gave him a place in his military family. Upon the duties of his new position he enterered with characteristic vigor, and in the assault upon Quebec led a forlorn hope of forty men. He stood near Montgomery when he fell, but escaped being taken prisoner.† And

---

*" From our last lodgings [Sartigan] hired a peasant, and proceeded down the river in a canoe five miles to a victualing house, or other place of rendezvous. This village, St. Josephs, made a further agreement, and continued down the river about four miles further, as we found nothing agreeable since our arrival, except one quart of New England rum, (if that was to be allowed so,) for which I paid one hard dollar. We were making enquiry at every likely stage; for this purpose visited an old peasant's house, where was a merry old woman at her loom, and two or three fine young girls. They were exceedingly rejoiced with our company. Bought some eggs, rum, sugar, sweetmeats, &c., where we made ourselves very happy. Upon the old woman being acquainted from whence we came, [she] immediately fell singing and dancing "Yankee Doodle" with the greatest air of good humour. After making the old woman satisfied for her kickshaws, saluted her for her civilities, &c., marched. The distance computed from the Chaudiere Lake to the inhabitants, one hundred miles. From thence to Quebec, ninety."—*Senter's Journal.*

†Colonel Trumbull, in his great national painting, represents General Montgomery as falling into Burr's arms.

thus was opened to an ambitious young man, resembling, in some qualities of character, his commander Arnold, a career of high promise, destined however, as the sequel proved, to an unhappy blight. Having achieved a distinguished military reputation, and after filling the position of Vice-President of the United States, he closed an eventful life with a cloud resting upon his name.†

Pressing forward in defiance of all untoward circumstances, Arnold and his devoted band, now reduced to about 550 effective men, reached Point Levi on the 8th November, crossed the St. Lawrence with the aid of thirty-five canoes on the 13th, and advancing to the Plains of Abraham, sat down in defiant attitude before Quebec. On the 14th, Arnold sent a flag with a letter to Lieut. Governor Cramahé, demanding the surrender of the city. The officer bearing the flag, on approaching the walls was fired upon, and narrowly escaped being killed. The officer retired from his perilous position. A second flag was sent, with a similar result. This method of refusing to receive a flag, so contrary to military usage, called forth an indignant letter from Arnold, in which he threatened the British commander with retaliation. On the 18th he inspected the condition of the arms and ammunition of his little army, and found that a great part of the cartridges were unfit for service, leaving not more than five rounds for each man, while one hundred muskets, or about one-fifth of the whole, proved to be worthless for present use. In the mean time, he had ascertained that the garrison of the enemy had been augmented to about seven hundred men—and soon swelled to about nineteen hundred—a force too large to justify an immediate attempt to storm the city. It was deemed therefore prudent to fall back to Point-aux-Trembles, and await the arrival of General Montgomery. This, after trying in vain to draw the enemy into the open field, was done, Nov. 19th.

The work undertaken by General Montgomery was environed with no ordinary difficulties. He had not only to contend with the rigors of a Canadian winter,—with the small pox and other forms of disease which ravaged his camp and threatened more destruction than was to be apprehended from the enemy, but also to compose the dissentions that had sprung up among his officers, and to allay the spirit of disaffection they had spread among the men, which presaged ruin to the campaign. But he showed himself equal to the emergency, and under all these unpromising circumstances continued his advance from Montreal. On the 3d December he formed a junction with Arnold at Point-aux-Trembles and the next day the united forces appeared before Quebec. On the 6th General Montgomery sent a flag of truce to Governor Carleton, summoning a surrender. The flag he refused to receive, declaring that he would hold no parley with rebels. Batteries were established within striking distance of the walls, protected by breastworks of snow, converted into solid ice by pouring water upon it. But it was soon found that the metal thrown by the artillery was too light to breach the walls or do any essential damage inside.* Here the dissensions before mentioned again broke out, which necessitated a change in the original plan of attack. December 31st had been fixed upon for making an assault. Early in the morning of that day the army, now only eight hundred strong, began to move in two columns upon the Lower Town. The first, led by Montgomery, was to make an attack at Cape Diamond, while the second, under Arnold, was to attack through St. Roque. The assaults were made with great vigor, but with disaster to the American cause. General Montgomery

---

†To the Lives of Burr written by Davis, Knapp and Parton, the reader is referred for details of an extraordinary man.

*"I never expected any other advantage from our artillery than to amuse the enemy and blind them to my real intention."—*Montgomery to General Wooster.*

early fell mortally wounded, while aiding in removing the pickets at Cape Diamond, for the ingress of his men. Arnold's command carried a two-gun battery, which the enemy bravely defended for an hour. In this attack he was shot through the leg, and was compelled to retire from the field,* while his men pushed on to a second barrier, which they took, but not without severe loss. The enemy had the advantage of the ground in front, a vast superiority of numbers, and dry and better arms, which gave them an irresistible power in so narrow a space. Humphreys, upon a mound, which was speedily erected, attended by many brave men, attempted to scale the barrier, but was compelled to retreat by the formidable phalanx of bayonets within, and the weight of fire from the platform and the adjacent buildings. Morgan, brave to temerity, stormed and raged. Hendricks, Steele, Nichols and Humphrey, equally brave, were calm, though under a tremendous fire. Hendricks, when aiming his rifle, received a ball through his heart, and instantly expired. Humphrey, of Virginia, in like manner received a death wound. Lieut. Cooper, of Connecticut, was killed. Captain Lamb had a portion of his face carried away by a grape or canister shot. Lieut. Steele lost three of his fingers as he was presenting his gun to fire. Captain Hubbard and Lieut. Tisdale were also among the wounded.† The battle raged fiercely for the space of four and a half hours, when a sudden sally of the enemy from the Palace gate upon their rear, forced the surrender of such of Arnold's men as could not effect an escape. Thus, in one brief half day, vanished the brilliant anticipations of the preceding three months.'

The number of killed, wounded, and taken prisoners in this battle has been variously stated, and may not as yet be definitely certain. Immediately after the fight, General Carleton reported the American loss in killed and wounded to be one hundred. Major Meigs estimated the loss at the same number. A school history fixes the killed at 160, and the prisoners at 426. Ware gives a list of names, and sums up results as follows: Killed, 48; wounded, 34; taken prisoners, 372; total, 454. This is more reliable than any statement that has previously been made. Yet this list may not include all of either class. Of the company with which Captain Thayer started from Cambridge, 22 were sent back from the wilderness sick, 11 were killed at Quebec, 27 including himself were taken prisoners, 3 deserted, 8 enlisted in the King's service, 3 entered on board a man-of-war, and 2 on board fishermen, leaving 8 as escaped, or to be otherwise accounted for. Of Captain Morgan's company, less than twenty-five regained their native homes. "Our loss and repulse," says Arnold, in a letter to Washington, "struck an amazing panic into both officers and men, and had the enemy improved their advantage, our affairs here must have been

* "Daylight had scarce made its appearance, ere Colonel Arnold was brought in supported by two soldiers, wounded in the leg with a piece of a musket ball. The ball had probably come in contact with a cannon, rock, stone or the like, ere it entered the leg which had cleft off nigh a third. The other two-thirds entered the outer side of the leg, about midway, and in an oblique course passed between the tibia and fibula, lodged in the gastrocnemeus muscle at the rise of the tendon achilles, where upon examination I easily discovered and extracted it. Before the Colonel was done with, Major Ogden came in wounded through the left shoulder, which proved only a flesh wound.

"We were momentarily expecting them [the enemy] out upon us, as we concluded Arnold's division, then under the command of Lieut. Col. Greene, were all killed, captured, &c. Under these circumstances, we entreated Colonel Arnold for his own safety to be carried back into the country where they would not readily find him when out, but to no purpose. He would neither be removed nor suffer a man from the Hospital to retreat. He ordered his pistols loaded, with a sword on his bed, &c., adding that he was determined to kill as many as possible if they came into the room. We were now all soldiers, even to the wounded in their beds were ordered a gun by their side."—*Dr. Senter's Journal.*

† Henry, pp. 117-119.

entirely ruined. It was not in my power to prevail on the officers to attempt saving our morters, which had been placed in St. Roque's. Of course they fell into the hands of the enemy. Upwards of one hundred officers and soldiers instantly set off for Montreal, and it was with the greatest difficulty I could persuade the rest to make a stand."

"During the night of the attack on Quebec, there was a tempestuous snow-storm. The bodies of the persons slain under the cliff of Cape Diamond, were not discovered till morning, when they were found nearly enveloped in snow. They were taken into the city on a sled. Three of them were known to the officers, and from the initials R. M. written in a fur cap, picked up at the place of the bloody catastrophe, it was conjectured to have belonged to General Montgomery. His features were disfigured by a wound, which he had received in the lower part of the head and neck. At length a woman and a boy were brought, who had lately come into the city from the American camp, and who had often seen the principal officers. They identified the bodies of Montgomery, Captain McPherson, Captain Cheeseman, and an Orderly Sergeant.

Mr. Cramahé, an officer in the British army, and for a time Lieutenant-Governor of Canada, had served in the late [French] war with Montgomery, and entertained for him a warm personal attachment. He asked permission of General Carleton to bury his friend with marks of honor and respect. This was granted in part, and a coffin lined with black was provided. But the Governor did not consent to the reading of the funeral service, probably not deeming this indulgence conformable to military rules. But when the time of burial approached, Mr. Cramahé invited a clergyman [Rev. Mr. de Montmolin,] to be present, who read the service privately and unmolested."*

General Montgomery was buried on the evening of January 4th, near the ramparts bounding on St. Louis-Gate. There the body rested until June, 1818, when it was exhumed and conveyed to the city of New York, and reïnterred with the highest civil and military honors. The General's sword, after he fell, was taken by James Thompson, a citizen of Quebec, who served in the capacity of Assistant Engineer during the siege of the city, by whom it was worn until going one day to the Seminary where the American officers were lodged, they recognized it and were moved to tears. Out of respect to their feelings he laid it aside, and never wore it more. The General's knee buckles were given by Major McKenzie to Major Meigs, as was also a gold broach that belonged to Capt. McPherson. Both the General's aides, Captains McPherson and Cheeseman, were buried in their clothes without coffins, and in the military manner.

Several circumstances combined to render this attack unsuccessful. In the first place, the Indian Messenger by whom Colonel Arnold, while on his march, forwarded a letter to Mr. Mercier, of Montreal, proved treacherous, and delivered it to the Lieutenant Governor, thereby revealing impending danger, and affording about twenty days' time to put the city of Quebec in a state of defence. Then there was a delay of several days after arriving at Point Levi, opposite Quebec, in getting all the troops across the river, the enemy (apprised of their approach) having destroyed all the canoes upon which Arnold had relied, at that point. This delay enabled the Governor to avail of the services of one hundred men, chiefly carpenters, who arrived in a vessel from Newfoundland November 5th, in repairing the defences, and in making platforms for the cannon. It also afforded time for Colonel Maclean to reach the city with 170 men of his regiment, with which to man the fortifications. This was a very important fact in its bearings upon the general ope-

*Spark's Washington, iii, p. 254, note.

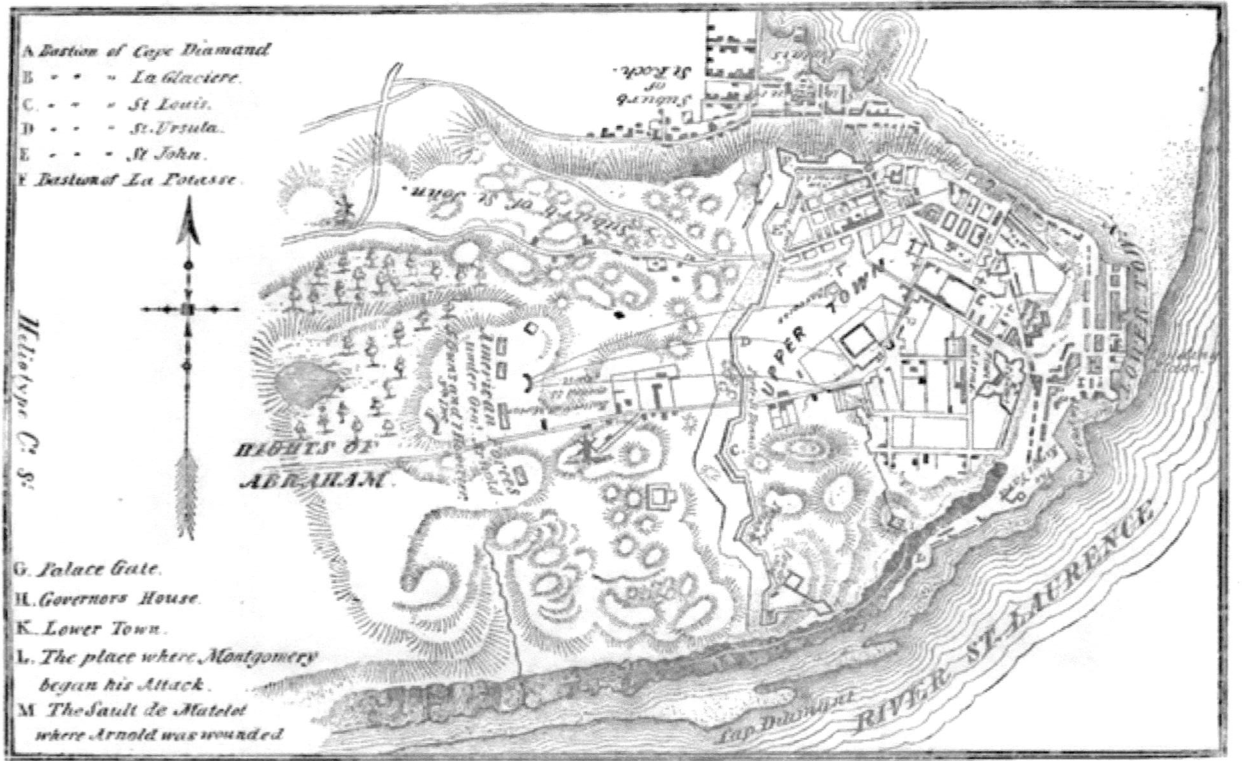

COL. ARNOLD'S FORCES BEFORE QUEBEC, 1775.

rations; for up to Nov. 5th, when Arnold's forces were at St. Mary's, thirty miles from Quebec, there was not a soldier in the city, and had he pushed on and reached there on the 10th, with even half his force, the gates of the city would have been opened to him. Then, finally, the death of General Montgomery and his own wounded condition changed the situation of affairs at a critical moment, and that portion of the troops led by General Montgomery having retreated after his fall, gave the enemy an opportunity to turn their whole force and attention upon those who remained still fighting. To contend longer with superior numbers was only to sacrifice life without an equivalent; and after a sortie by the enemy, in which they captured an entire company, and retreat appeared impracticable, surrender or annihilation became inevitable. The first of these alternatives was chosen, and after maintaining their ground from 5½ o'clock until 10 o'clock, A. M., the gallant band gave themselves up prisoners of war.

The death of General Montgomery devolved the command of the assaulting forces upon Colonel Arnold, but he being already wounded was unable to act, and temporarily gave the command to Colonel Campbell. The day following the repulse, Arnold assumed the position that disaster had assigned him, and in the midst of excessive pain from his wound, began to plan for retrieving the fortunes of his little army. On the 10th of January, Congress appointed him Brigadier General, as a reward for his good conduct during the march and before Quebec.

The energy displayed by Arnold, and the fortitude shown by his men, extorted expressions of admiration from an English writer describing the occurrences of that remarkable campaign. "Their perseverance," he says, "was astonishing in their circumstances. They had lost beside their General, (in whom it might be said all their hopes and confidence resided,) the best of their own officers, and the bravest of their fellows, with a part of their small artillery. The hope of assistance was distant, and at best, the arrival of succors must be slow. It was well known that the Canadians, besides being naturally quick and fickle in their resolutions, were peculiarly disposed to be biased by success, so that their assistance now grew extremely precarious. The severity of a Canadian winter was also far beyond anything they were acquainted with, and the snow lay about five feet deep upon a level. In these circumstances, it required no small share of activity, as well as address, to keep them in any manner together. Arnold, who had hitherto displayed uncommon talents in his march into Canada, (which may be compared to the greatest things done in that kind) discovered on this occasion the utmost vigor of a determined mind, and a genius full of resources. Defeated and wounded as he was, he put his troops into such a situation as to keep them formidable."*

Arnold wrote to Washington from Quebec, on the 27th of February, and seemed in high spirits, though encompassed with innumerable difficulties. His mind was of so elastic a nature, that the more it was pressed, the greater was its power of resistance." The severity of the climate," he observes, "the troops very ill clad and worse paid, the trouble of reconciling matters among the inhabitants,† and lately

*Annual Register, 1776, p. 16.

† One difficulty experienced by the American Army grew out of the scarcity of hard money in the Paymaster's Exchequer, and for which Continental paper money was substituted. Of this the inhabitants of Canada were distrustful, and were unwilling to receive it in payment for supplies, especially as army drafts had frequently been dishonored. When this currency was forced upon them as their only alternative, it is not surprising that a feeling akin to indignation should have been excited. An actor in the scenes of the Canadian campaign writes: "Our Continental Money required *a good deal of gesticulation* to make it go. It was not much relished by our Canadian friends, at its par value. One of my amusements was to play tricks upon an old market woman, who retailed articles out of a dog-cart, still a vehicle of great repute in Canada. Her shrill voice, and exclamations of voia (voila) mauvay (mauvais) Bostony! still haunt my memory."—*The Scrogenary*, p. 46.

an uneasiness among some of the New York and other officers, who think themselves neglected in the new arrangement, while those who deserted the cause and went home last fall have been promoted; in short, the choice of difficulties I have had to encounter has rendered affairs so perplexing, that I have often been at a loss how to conduct them." He alludes here, and perhaps with some justice, to the case of Colonel Enos, and his officers, who as already mentioned, deserted him in the wilderness on their way to Canada, but were nevertheless retained and promoted in the new establishment.*

This disastrous repulse did not crush out hope of ultimate success. "Quebec appears to me," writes Arnold to the Continental Congress, "an object of the highest importance to the Colonies, and, if proper methods are adopted, must inevitably fall into their hands before the garrison can be relieved." He adds, "I beg leave to recommend the sending a body of at least five thousand men, with an experienced General, into Canada as early as possible; and in the mean time that every possible preparation of mortars, howitzers, and some heavy cannon should be made, as the season will permit our raising batteries by the middle of March; which may very possibly be attended with success, as we can place our mortars under cover within two hundred yards of the walls, and within one thousand feet of the centre of the town."† In his future, Arnold calculated largely on the good will of the citizens, who were supposed to be friendly to his success. "I am well assured," he says, "more than one-half of the inhabitants of Quebec would gladly open the gates to us, but are prevented by the strict discipline and watch kept over them; the command of the guards being constantly given to officers of the Crown known to be firm in their interest. The garrison consists of about fifteen hundred men, great part of whom Governor Carleton can place no confidence in, or he would not suffer a blockade, and every distress of a siege, by seven hundred men, our force consisting of no more at present, including Colonel Livingston's regiment of two hundred Canadians."

Washington warmly sympathized with the determined persistent spirit of Arnold, and had it been in his power would gladly have given him the reënforcements he desired.‡ "It would give me great pleasure," he said, "if I could be the happy

---

* Sparks.

† "The 22d of this month [January] a battery opened from the bank of Charles river, by name of Smith's battery. From this was discharged red hot shot, in hopes of firing the town. They returned the fire exceeding heavy, but no considerable harm from either side. Two of our artillery-men were wounded very much by the cartridges taking fire while ramming them home, but recovered again. The enemy continued their cannonade and bombardment excessive heavy, while we were restricted to a certain number per day, in consequence of very little ammunition. There was very little damage from either cannon or bombs."—*Senter.*

‡ *January* 27, 1776, Washington wrote to Arnold: "I need not mention to you the great importance of this place, and the consequent possession of all Canada, in the scale of American affairs. You are well apprised of it. To whomsoever it belongs, in their favor, probably, will the balance turn. If it is in ours, success I think will most certainly crown our virtuous struggles. If it is in theirs, the contest at best will be doubtful, hazardous, and bloody. The glorious work must be accomplished in the course of this winter, otherwise it will become difficult, most probably impracticable; for administration, knowing that it will be impossible ever to reduce us to a state of slavery and arbitrary rule without it, will certainly send a large re-enforcement thither in the spring. I am fully convinced that your exertions will be invariably directed to this grand object, and I already view the approaching day, when you and your brave followers will enter this important fortress, with every honor attendant on victory. Then will you have added the only link wanting in the great chain of Continental union, and render the freedom of your country secure." The confident expectations here expressed were destined five months later to be sadly disappointed.

means of relieving our fellow-citizens now in Canada, and prevent the ministerial troops from exulting long, and availing themselves of the advantages arising from this repulse. But it is not in my power. Since the dissolution of the old army, the progress in raising recruits for the new has been so very slow and inconsiderable, that five thousand militia have been called for the defence of our lines. A great part of these have gone home again, and the rest have been induced to stay with the utmost difficulty and persuasion, though their going would render the holding of the lines truly precarious and hazardous, in case of an attack. In short, I have not a man to spare."

But Washington was not idle. He called a council of general officers, who after due consideration of the importance of sustaining Arnold, "determined that the Colonies of Massachusetts, New Hampshire, and Connecticut should each immediately raise a regiment to continue in service for one year, and to march forthwith to Canada." Without waiting for Congress to carry out a resolution to raise nine battalions for that purpose, passed before the news of the failure of the attack on Quebec had reached them, Washington addressed letters to the General Court of Massachusetts, to the Governor of Connecticut and to the President of the Convention of New Hampshire, requesting them to act at once upon the decision of the war council. Connecticut had already anticipated the call, and sent off troops without delay to Canada, under the command of Colonel Warner. Other troops followed.

After the fall of Montgomery, General Schuyler was expected to repair to Canada, and take the chief command, but continued ill health and other causes induced him to decline going there. In February, 1776, General Lee was designated by Congress for that field, but was soon after transferred to the command of the Continental forces South of the Potomac, much to the gratification of Washington, who had already found him "fickle and violent." For a few months, General Wooster was the highest officer in Canada. On the 1st of April he took command of the army before Quebec, and on the day following, Arnold having received an injury from his horse falling upon him, retired on leave to Montreal for recovery.* May 1st, General Wooster gave place to General Thomas of Massachusetts. About this time a plot was formed to burn the shipping of the enemy in the harbor. A fire ship was completed in charge of Adjutant Anderson, a very brave officer, but proved abortive, by reason of the tide ebbing before he could get up to the shipping. The combustibles took fire before he intended, by which accident he was much burnt. He was, however, got on shore, and no lives were lost.†

When General Thomas arrived at the camp before Quebec, he found his army there to consist of 1900 men. Of these, only 1000 were fit for duty, officers included. The remainder were invalids, chiefly confined with the small pox. Three hundred of the effective were soldiers whose enlistments had expired. Many of these peremptorily refused duty, and all were importunate to return home. In all the magazines there were but one hundred and fifty pounds of powder, and not more

---

* February 15th, 1776, Congress appointed Dr. Franklin, Samuel Chase and Charles Carroll Commissioners to repair to Canada, and use all suitable means to induce the Canadians to join the other colonies in the contest with England. They were accompanied by Reverend John Carroll, afterwards Catholic Archbishop of Baltimore, whose influence with the people it was thought would be useful, on account of his religious principles and character. They arrived at Montreal April 29th, and used every effort in their power to accomplish the object of their mission, without success. Ill health caused Dr. Franklin to return in a few days. His associates remained till after the American forces had retreated to Sorel, and were preparing to evacuate Canada.—*Sparks.*

† Senter.

than six days provisions. The French inhabitants, too, were much disaffected, which rendered it more difficult to obtain supplies in the country.*

The state of blockade in which Arnold, immediately after the battle of December 31st, had placed Quebec, did not prevent re-enforcements being thrown into that city. Before the arrival of General Thomas the enemy had in their magazine more than 3000 barrels of powder, 10,000 stands of arms, and a large quantity of artillery stores. Two frigates and a number of other vessels were in the harbor, ready to render aid to the British garrison. On the 10th of May five more ships of war were added to the naval force of the enemy. The besieged, under Beaujean, attempted in March to raise the blockade, but failed. In May, however, a sally was made by the garrison upon the Continental forces, who were so dispersed that not more than two hundred men could be collected at head quarters, which compelled a retreat to the mouth of the Sorel. This was made in the utmost precipitation and confusion, with the loss of cannon, batteries, provisions, five hundred stands of small arms, and a batteau load of powder going down with Colonel Allen.† Two of the enemy's frigates proceeded immediately up the river, not only to annoy the retreating troops on their march, but also to seek several vessels of the fleet which General Montgomery brought from Montreal. Wind and tide favering the enemy's frigates, they were brought within cannon shot of the American vessels before they could get under way. They hauled upon our shipping so rapidly as to oblige the Captains to run them ashore, and set them on fire. They kept in pursuit up the river both by land and by water, increasing the disorder of the retreat.

The detachment stationed at Point Levi,‡ as well as those at Chairlebore, were not apprised of a retreat till they saw the Provincials quitting the ground. They were forced to escape through the woods a very great distance before they fell in with the St. Lawrence. Most of the sick fell into the hands of the enemy, with all the hospital stores, &c. The first stand made was at Chamband, forty-five miles from Quebec, but not being able to collect sufficient provisions, they were obliged to abandon the position and proceed. "The poor inhabitants, seeing the army abandoning their country, were in the utmost consternation, expecting, as many had been aiding us in every way, to be sacrificed to the barbarity of those whose severity they had long felt, though under the specious pretence of civil government, which, in fact, had been in essence nothing but an arrogant military one. No provisions could be obtained but by force of arms. No conveniences for ferrying the troops over the rivers emptying in upon either side of the St. Lawrence, except a canoe or two, and these were rare. The spring flood had submerged many low places, and the army was obliged to travel a great distance around them. In this

---

* Letter of General Thomas to Washington, May 8, 1776. On the same day, Arnold writes from Montreal: "We have very little provisions, no cash and less credit."

† The town of Sorel, or (as it is sometimes called) William Henry, stands on the site of a fort, built in the year 1665, by order of Mons. de Tracy. It was intended as a defence against the incursions of the Indians, and received its name of Sorel from a Captain of engineers, who superintended its construction.

The river Sorel is two hundred and fifty yards broad opposite to the town, but it presents a singular example of a river, much narrower at its embouchure than at its origin. It is more than four times as wide at St. John's, as at Sorel, and continues to widen all the way up the stream, to the Lake Champlain. From St. John's there is also a ship navigation into the lake; but from the town of Sorel, vessels of one hundred and fifty tons ascend only twelve or fourteen miles.—*Silliman's Tour.*

‡ Colonel Clinton, afterwards well known in our Revolution as a gallant general officer, and now not less remembered as the father of the illustrious DeWitt Clinton, commanded a battery at Point Levi. He afterwards commanded at Montreal.—*The Sexagenary, p. 44.*

perplexed situation, they arrived at Sorel, about forty miles below Montreal, where they made a stand and collected our whole force."*

At Sorel, General Thomas died of small pox.† On being taken sick, he sent for General Wooster, then at Montreal, to come and take the command, which for a short time he did. But General Sullivan was already on his way to Canada with re-enforcements, to join General Thomas, and the death of that officer devolved on him the command. He advanced to Sorel, where he established his head-quarters. His entire force consisted of about 3500 men, and he felt confident of soon being able to reduce Quebec. Writing to Washington in glowing strains, under date of June 5th, he says: "Our affairs here have taken a strange turn since our arrival. The Canadians are flocking by hundreds to take a part with ...

... we are." If we are not soon re-enforced, I tremble for the event. A loss of our heavy cannon, which is all ordered to Sorel, must ensue, if not of our army, as our retreat is far from being secured. Not one stroke has been struck to secure our encampment here. I have ordered men out to-morrow morning to inclose our encampment and the two old forts with an *abatis* and breastwork. Dr. Stringer is in a disagreeable situation. Three thousand men are sick here and at Chambly, and no room or convenience for them. I should advise his going to the Isle-aux-Noix, was there any convenience for the sick, or boards to make any."

than six days **provisions.** The French inhabitants, too, were much disaffected, which rendered it more difficult to obtain supplies in the country.*

The state of blockade in which Arnold, immediately after the battle of December 31st, had placed Quebec, did not prevent re-enforcements being thrown into that city. Before the arrival of General Thomas the enemy had in their magazine more than 3000 barrels of powder, 10,000 stands of arms, and a large quantity of artillery stores. Two frigates and a number of other vessels were in the harbor, ready to render aid to the British garrison. On the 10th of May five more ships of war were added to the naval force of the enemy. The besieged, under Beaujean, attempted [illegible] to raise the blockade, but failed. In May, however, a sally was made by [illegible] so dispersed that not more than

[The following should precede the death of General Thomas, mentioned at the top of page XXI.]

Colonel Bedel, with 350 continental troops, held a post at the Cedars, about forty three miles above Montreal. Learning on the 15th May that a party of the enemy consisting of about 600 regulars and Indians were marching to attack him, he set out for Montreal to obtain re-enforcements, leaving Major Butterfield in command. On the 17th, during his absence, the post was invested, and on the 19th contrary to the remonstrances of the officers, the fort and garrison were surrendered. On the 20th Major Sherburne with 100 men, landed at Quinze Chênes, about nine miles from the Cedars, where he was attacked by about 500 of the enemy, and after maintaining his ground for nearly an hour was constrained to retreat, but being intercepted on his route was, with his men, taken prisoner. The prisoners after the surrender, were treated with savage barbarity. One was shot and while yet alive, roasted, and others, worn down by famine and cruelty, were left exposed on an island to perish with cold and hunger. General Arnold advanced from Montreal to attack Quinze Chênes. Captain Foster, the English commander, sent a flag to meet him with a proposition to exchange prisoners, stating that if not complied with those in his possession would be exposed to merciless treatment from his savage allies, and to save them General Arnold reluctantly entered into a cartel, and the attack was not made. A Congressional Committee of Inquiry subsequently investigated the whole subject, and reported that "the shameful surrender of the post at the Cedars was chargeable on the commanding officer." Congress also condemned in severe terms the cruelties practiced upon the American prisoners, and other violations of the comity of war.*

* Proceedings of Congress, 1776.

The river Sorel is two hundred and [illegible] than at its origin. It is a singular example of a river, much narrower at its embouchure than at its origin. It is more than four times as wide at St. John's, as at Sorel, and continues to widen all the way up the stream, to the Lake Champlain. From St. John's there is also a ship navigation into the lake; but from the town of Sorel, vessels of one hundred and fifty tons ascend only twelve or fourteen miles.—*Silliman's Tour.*

‡ Colonel Clinton, afterwards well known in our Revolution as a gallant general officer, and now not less remembered as the father of the illustrious DeWitt Clinton, commanded a battery at Point Levi. He afterwards commanded at Montreal.—*The Seragenary, p. 44.*

perplexed situation, they arrived at Sorel, about forty miles below Montreal, where they made a stand and collected our whole forces."*

At Sorel, General Thomas died of small pox.† On being taken sick, he sent for General Wooster, then at Montreal, to come and take the command, which for a short time he did. But General Sullivan was already on his way to Canada with re-enforcements, to join General Thomas, and the death of that officer devolved on him the command. He advanced to Sorel, where he established his head-quarters. His entire force consisted of about 3500 men, and he felt confident of soon being able to reduce Quebec. Writing to Washington in glowing strains, under date of June 5th, he says: "Our affairs here have taken a strange turn since our arrival. The Canadians are flocking by hundreds to take a part with us. I am giving them commissions agreeable to the enclosed form, which I hope will not be thought an unnecessary assumption of power. I really find most of them exceedingly friendly. I have sent out for carts and teams, &c. They have come in with the greatest cheerfulness; and, what gives still greater evidence of their friendship is, that they have voluntarily offered to supply us with what wheat, flour, &c., we want, and ask nothing in return but certificates. They begin to complain against their priests, and wish them to be secured; I shall, however, touch this string with great tenderness at present, as I know their sacerdotal influence."

Either General Sullivan was greatly deceived by appearances, or had been grossly imposed upon by false professions. At any rate, two weeks sufficed to cloud these bright skies, and doom him to disappointment. Two days after his arrival at Sorel, he sent General Thompson with three regiments to attack the enemy at Three Rivers, but unfortunately for the enterprise Burgoyne arrived the night before the battle, with a strong party. General Thompson was defeated and with other officers was taken prisoner. The fortunes of war were now against Sullivan. There was a want of almost every necessary for the army, while repeated misfortunes and losses had greatly dispirited the troops. The British land force had not only been heavily strengthened, but they had thirty-six sail of vessels lying in the lake near Sorel, and sixty-six more lying at Three Rivers. The numbers under the command of Sullivan were entirely inadequate to the work he had undertaken, while "small pox, famine and disorder, had rendered them almost lifeless." The warmth of Canadian friendship, which had been so conspicuous when Montgomery crossed the line seven months before, and so suddenly cooled after the disaster at Quebec, which rose again to summer heat on the appearance of Sullivan, now sank to zero. The fickle population changed with every turn of fortune. Success was the price to be paid for their good will. From a doubtful cause they withheld support. Every day the situation of affairs became more precarious, and in view of all circumstances, a council of war decided upon an entire withdrawal from Canada.

---

* Dr. Senter.

† June 13, 1776, Arnold wrote from St. John's to General Schuyler as follows: "Near one-half of our army are sick, mostly with the small pox. If the enemy have a force of six or eight, and some say ten thousand men, we shall not be able to oppose them, sick, divided, ragged, undisciplined, and unofficered, as we are. If we are not soon re-enforced, I tremble for the event. A loss of our heavy cannon, which is all ordered to Sorel, must ensue, if not of our army, as our retreat is far from being secured. Not one stroke has been struck to secure our encampment here. I have ordered men out to-morrow morning to inclose our encampment and the two old forts with an *abatis* and breastwork. Dr. Stringer is in a disagreeable situation. Three thousand men are sick here and at Chambly, and no room or conveniences for them. I should advise his going to the Isle-aux-Noix, was there any convenience for the sick, or boards to make any."

This was effected about the middle of June in an orderly manner, without loss of men, armament or baggage.*

On the 17th of June, before this event was known, Congress directed General Washington to send General Gates to Canada to assume the chief command. Gates had then a popular military reputation, and strong hopes were entertained that he would soon be able to give a successful turn to affairs. Receiving his instructions in New York, he proceeded June 3d, by way of Albany to Ticonderoga. But the evacuation of Canada, which had already taken place, put an end to a project that for more than nine months had occupied the attention of Congress, and which had given great anxiety to Washington.

The termination of the invasion of Canada, so differently from universal expectation, was a deep disappointment to the country. Life, treasure and time seemed to have been expended in vain.† Yet this expenditure was not wholly without compensation. The experience gained was calculated to toughen the will, and to make more energetic soldiers of both officers and men. Besides, viewing the result through the medium of subsequent events, it is questionable whether the possession of Canada at that time would have secured to the Continental Confederacy the advantages then anticipated. It has been said, with much plausibility, that had Quebec fallen, while it would have seemed a most important and glorious event, yet it might have been the ruin of America; for in order to defend it, a considerable force would have been requisite, thus dividing our strength, while the British, in despair of recovering so strong a place, might have concentrated their forces at New York, and the capture of Burgoyne would not have electrified the friends of liberty through America.‡

But however this may be, the plan of wresting Canada from Great Britain, and giving the blessings of freedom to its people, was a grand conception, while the record of the manly fortitude displayed by the army under the most trying circumstances, is a noble monument to its patriotism. The simple, unambitious story told in the following Journal, well illustrates the spirit that fired the army of the Revolution, and shows, in vivid light, how much our ancestors were ready to endure to secure for their posterity the boon of human rights. It has been truly said, "The long, difficult and laborious march of Arnold through hardships and dangers

---

* "I advised General Sullivan to secure his retreat by retiring to St. John's. He was determined to keep his post at Sorel, if possible, and did not retire until the 14th [June] instant, at which time the enemy were as high up with their ships as the Sorel.

On the 15th at night, when the enemy were at twelve miles distant from me, I quitted Montreal with my little garrison of three hundred men. The whole army with their baggage and cannon (except three heavy pieces left at Chambly,) arrived at St. John's the 17th, and at the Isle-aux-Noix the 18th; previous to which it was determined by a Council of War at St. John's, that in our distressed situation, (one-half of the army sick, and almost the whole destitute of clothing and every necessary of life, except salt pork and flour,) it was not only imprudent but impracticable to keep possession of St. John's, Crown Point was judged the only place of health and safety, to which the army could retire and oppose the enemy. It was found necessary to remain at the Isle-aux-Noix for some few days, until the sick, heavy cannon, &c., could be removed."—*Arnold to General Washington, June 25, 1776.*

† "The loss of Canada," writes Hancock, President of Congress, "is undoubtedly on some accounts to be viewed in the light of a misfortune. The Continent has been put to a great expense in endeavoring to get possession of it. That our army should make so prudent a retreat, as to save their baggage, cannon, ammunition and sick from falling into the hands of the enemy, is a circumstance that will afford a partial consolation, and reflect honor upon the officers who conducted it."

‡ Allen.

that would have appalled the stoutest follower of Xenophon—his subsequent siege and blockade of one of the strongest military posts in the world, in the heart of the enemy's country, in the midst of a northern winter, where nothing was seen but ice and snow, with raw recruits, half clad, half fed, and scarcely half covered from the storms of wind and snow—the expedition to Canada may fairly be placed on a parallel with any of the boasted achievements of ancient Greece or Rome." We turn painfully away from Arnold's display of patriotic devotion in this marvelous march, and before Quebec, as we remember his base and heartless treachery at West Point. How sad, that a life of such glorious promise should have draped itself forever in a robe of infamy!

NOTES.

Death of General Montgomery. Page xvi.

"Some American gentlemen who were at Quebec about sixteen years since, saw a man who asserted that he was the person who touched off the cannon, and what was very remarkable he was a New Englander. He related that the barrier was abandoned, and that the party who had been stationed at it were in full flight; but as it occurred to him that there was a loaded cannon, he turned, and discharged it at random, and then ran. This anecdote I had from one of the gentlemen who conversed with this man.

That there was some such occurrence, appears probable, and the following circumstances having a similar bearing, were related to me by the person who showed me this fatal ground. The spot may be known at the present moment, by its being somewhat farther up the river than the naval depot, where great numbers of heavy cannon are now lying. The battery stood on the first gentle declivity, beyond this pile of cannon, and the deaths happened on the level ground, about forty yards still farther on. My informant stated that the people in the block-house, as he called it, loaded their cannon over night, and retired to rest. It so happened, (and it was perfectly accidental,) that a Captain of a vessel in the port, lodged in the block-house that night. He was an intemperate man, half delirious when most sober, and never minded any one or was much listened to by others. Early on the fatal morning, before light, he exclaimed, all of a sudden,—" they are coming, I s——r they are coming." No one regarded him, but he got the iron rods, which they used to touch off the cannon, heated them, and fired the pieces. Immediately sky rockets were seen to fly into the air, which were signals to Arnold's party that all was lost. When light returned, General Montgomery and his aids and many others, in the whole twenty-seven (as he stated,) were found either dead or grievously wounded."—*Silliman's Tour*, 1819.

Washington to Arnold on the Death of Montgomery.

Cambridge, 27th January, 1776.

Dear Sir:

On the 17th instant I received the melancholy account of the unfortunate attack on the city of Quebec, attended with the fall of General Montgomery and other brave officers and men, and of your being wounded.

This unhappy affair affects me in a very sensible manner, and I sincerely condole with you upon the occasion; but, in the midst of distress, I am happy to find that suitable honors were paid to the remains of Mr. Montgomery; and that our officers and soldiers, who have fallen into their hands, were treated with kindness and humanity.

Colonel Arnold's Account of the Attack on Quebec, in a Letter to General Wooster.

General Hospital, 31 December, 1775.

Dear Sir:—I make no doubt but General Montgomery acquainted you with his intentions of storming Quebec as soon as a good opportunity offered. As we had several men deserted from us a few days past, the General was induced to alter his plan, which was to have attacked the Upper and Lower Town at the same time. He thought it most prudent to make two different attacks upon the Lower Town; the one at Cape Diamond, the other through St. Roc. For the last attack, I was ordered with my own detachment and Captain Lamb's company of artillery. At five o'clock, the hour appointed for the attack, a false attack was ordered to be made upon the Upper Town.

We accordingly began our march. I passed through St. Roc, and approached near a two-gun battery, picketed in, without being discovered, which we attacked. It was bravely defended for about an hour; but with the loss of a number of men, we carried it. In the attack, I was shot through the leg, and was obliged to be carried to the hospital, where I soon heard the disagreeable news that the General was defeated at Cape Diamond; himself, Captain Macpherson, his Aide de Camp, and Captain Cheeseman, killed on the spot, with a number of others not known. After gaining the battery, my detachment pushed on to a second barrier, which they took possession of. At the same time, the enemy sallied out from Palace Gate, and attacked them in the rear. A field-piece, which the roughness of the road would not permit our carrying on, fell into the enemy's hands, with a number of prisoners. The last accounts from my detachment, about ten minutes since, they were pushing for the Lower Town. Their communication with me was cut off. I am exceedingly apprehensive what the event will be; they will either carry the Lower Town, be made prisoners, or cut to pieces.

I thought proper to send an express to let you know the critical situation we are in, and make no doubt you will give us all the assistance in your power. As I am not able to act, I shall give up the command to Colonel Campbell. I beg you will immediately send an express to the Honorable Continental Congress, and His Excellency General Washington. The loss of my detachment before I left it, was about twenty men killed and wounded; among the latter is Major Ogden, who, with Captain Oswald, Captain Burr, and the other volunteers, behaved extremely well. I have only time to add that I am, with the greatest esteem, &c.,

BENEDICT ARNOLD.

P. S. It is impossible to say what our future operations will be until we know the fate of my detachment.

PAGE XX.

January 6, 1776.—A battery opened from Point Levi upon the city, but being scanty of ammunition, were allowanced only a few rounds per day, just to keep the enemy in a continued alarm. About this time an insurrection happened down the river St. Lawrence, about six leagues from Quebec, in consequence of some of the enemy's emissaries, joined to the envious instigations of some of their priests. They collected a number of Canadians, and were marching up in form to take possession of our troops at Point Levi. Of this the General obtained intelligence, and immediately detached Major Dubois, a very brave officer, with a number of men to oppose them. The Major fell in with their party upon surprise, killed some, wounded others, (among the last was a priest) and captured a number more and brought them to Headquarters.—*Senter.*

JOURNAL.

A Journal of the indefatigable march of Col. Benedict Arnold from Prospect Hill Fort, in order to join the detachment which was going on a secret expedition, consisting of two Battalions, one commanded by Lieut. Col. Greene, and the other by Lieut. Col. Enos, with all circumstances, and particularly the difficulties that I myself have labored under, having the command of a company of Foot under Lieut. Col. Greene, in the years 1775 and 1776.

The first Battalion consisted of
1 Lieut. Colonel, (Greene,) 1 Major,
1 Adjutant, 1 Quartermaster.

The second Battalion consisted of
1 Lieut. Colonel, (Enos,) 1 Major,
1 Adjutant, 1 Quartermaster.
1 Surgeon and Mate for both Battalions.

Captain Smith's Company,
" Hendrick's "
" Ward's "
" Topham's "
" McCobb's "
" Hubbard's "
" Thayer's "

Captain Morgan's Company,
" Williams' "
" Hanchet's "
" Goodrich's "
" Dearborn's "
" Scott's "

One Chief Colonel, 1 Chaplain for both Battalions.

MARCH TO NEWBURYPORT.

Sept. 11.—Remained in Cambridge in order to fill up each company to 84 effective men. Got all necessaries and began our march.

Sept. 13.—This day our Battalion marched towards Newburyport, reached Beverly and remained there this night.

Sept. 14.—Continued our march and reached Malden and lodged there.

Sept. 15.—Arrived at Newburyport about sunset, and quartered our men in the Presbyterian Meeting House. [See Appendix A.]

Sept. 16.—Capt. Topham's company, together with mine, arrived.

Sept. 17.—Being Sunday we paraded our men, and went to meeting under arms,* after which we had orders to hold ourselves in readiness to embark at a moment's warning, in eleven small vessels purposely engaged to receive us on Board. Agreeable to orders we embarked about sunset, But finding it difficult to keep the men on board, we were obliged to keep a guard over them.

Sept. 18.—About 9 o'clock the fleet sailed for Kennebeck River, bearing W. S. W., got over the bar, and stood off until Col. Arnold came on board the Broad Bay schooner where little after the swallow Sloop struck a Rock where she stuck, on board of which was Capt. Scott's company who were distributed among the fleet, and Capt. Hendrick's company of Riflemen, together with mine, which were on board the Broad Bay. At 2 o'clock a signal was made for sailing, and run along shore until midnight, when a signal was given for heaving to, off the shore, under our jib and mainsail.

Sept. 19.—About Daybreak, discover'd the mouth of the river, for which we stood in and anchor'd, tarried all Day for the fleet.

Sept. 20.—They all came up but the Conway and Abigail sloops. The weather, accompanied by a fog and heavy rain,

* At the Presbyterian Meeting-house, Rev. Jonathan Parsons.

blowed very fresh. Stood up the river, but the above sloops did not come up. [See Appendix B.]

Sept. 21.—Came to the head of Sheeps Gut River, out of which we discovered the missing vessels making sail, to our great satisfaction, on board of which were Capt. Topham's and my companys.

Sept. 22.—Went on shore with Col. Arnold at Capt. Copelins, where there were one hundred men to row the Batteaux to Fort Western.

Sept. 23.—Proceeded to Fort Western.* This place was formerly pretty strong; was built against the French and Indians, but at present of no great consequence. It has two large and two small block houses.

Sept. 24.—Occupied in getting our men and Provisions up from Gardner's Town. After Capt. Topham and myself went to bed at a neighbor's house, some dispute arose in the house between some of our soldiers, on which we were requested to get up and appease them. I got out of Bed, and ordered them to lie down and be at rest; and on going to the door, I observed the flash of the priming of a gun, and called to Capt. Topham who arose likewise and went to the door, was fired at, but was miss'd, on which he drew back, and I with Topham went to bed, but the felon who had fully determined murder in his heart, came again to the door and lifted the latch, and fired into the room, and killed a man lying by the fireside. On suspicion, we took up a man, but did not prove to be the murderer.

Sept. 25.—The perpetrator of the above facts was taken by a Sergeant, who, thinking he was a deserter, questioned him accordingly, and who came to understand that he crossed the river opposite to the place where he killed the man, and gave himself up to the mercy of the Sergeant, who brought him back and was sentenced to die. This afternoon an advanced guard went forward, consisting of four Batteaux. This day the three companies of Riflemen sat off for Quebec, the place of our destination, and Col. Greene's Battalion received orders to be ready at a minute's warning.

* Opposite the present town of Augusta.

Sept. 26.—We began our march. The above perpetrator, by name Jn° McCormick, was to suffer at 3 o'clock, but was reprieved at that time to be sent back to Gen. Washington. The river here is very rapid and difficult. [See Appendix C.]

Sept. 27.—Arrived at Fort Halifax about 3 o'clock, P. M., which greatly resembles Fort Western. The river here is both rapid and rocky. Proceeded to the foot of the falls. Here is the first carrying place we come to. We encamped on the west side of the river, and carried over our provisions and Batteaux. The carrying place is about eighty rods wide.

Sept. 28.—Proceeded about 3 miles through rapid water. Our men are obliged to wade more than half their time. It begins to be cold and uncomfortable. Here are few scattering inhabitants. [See Appendix D.]

Sept. 29.—Proceeded on our march; made large fires and refreshed ourselves. Our People are in good health, But some keep lurking behind and get lost from the party. At 12 o'clock, set out again for Squhegan* Falls; the stream is very swift, which makes it difficult, and our Batteaux leaky, besides the place being very shallow, which obliges our men to go into the river and haul the Batteaux after them, which generally occupies three or four men, two of whom are at her head and one or two at her stern, which occasioned a slow progress. To-night we encamped within three miles of the falls, the water still continues to run very rapid.

Sept. 30.—Proceeded through the falls in rapid water; here is the second carrying place. We found that the course of the river differ'd from the Draught we had seen. We encamped on the main on the west side of the river. The carrying place is across an island. Here is a mill erecting, (the property of Mr. Copelin,) the worst constructed I ever saw. The People call this place Canaan; a Canaan, Indeed! The land is good, the timber large and of various kinds, such as Pine, Oak, Hemlock and Rock Maple. Last night, our clothes being wet, were frozen a pane of glass thick, which proved very disagreeable, being obliged to lie in them. The land is very fine, and am thinking if worked up, would produce any grain

* Skowhegan.

whatsoever. The people are courteous and breathe nothing but liberty. Their produce, (they sell at an exorbitant price) which consists of salted Moose and Deer, dried up like fish. They have Salmon in abundance. The cataracts here are neither so high nor so rapid as those at the fort, but narrow, which occasions the water below them to run very swift. The carrying place is very difficult, occasioned by the height of the land, and more so, being obliged to carry our provisions and Batteaux up a steep rocky precipice. Our men are as yet in very good spirits, considering they have to wade half the time, and our boats so villainously constructed, and leaking so much that they are always wet. I would heartily wish the infamous constructors, who, to satisfy their avaricious temper, and fill their purses with the spoils of their country, may be obliged to trust to the mercy of others more treacherous than themselves, that they might judge the fear and undergo the just reward of their villainy. This is the second carrying place.

Oct. 1.—Proceeded on our march seven miles. Stopped about an hour, advanced to Norridgewalk, and reached the falls about 12 o'clock and encamped on the west side of the river.*

Oct. 2.—This Day we saw an altar constructed by the Indians, and the remains of a Roman Chapel, where they paid their devotions. Their Curate, or Friar, named Francisco was killed about 40 years ago, at the time when the Provincials drove back the Indians. His remains lie buried here with a cross over them, as is customary in France, Spain, Italy and all Roman Catholic countries, when their clergy Die. This place was remarkable formerly for being the Indians' Headquarters. There we were busy in repairing our boats and carrying our Provisions over the carrying place, (the 3d) which is about one mile and a quarter long. We had some sleds and oxen to assist us in carrying our Luggage. We are at the Last inhabitants now, and meet no other until we come to Canada. Col. Arnold came up to us and encamped on the west side of the river. This is the fourth carrying place.

Oct. 3.—Overhauled our Biscuit and found it to be much

* See Appendix E.

damaged by the leaking of the Batteaux; passed the whole day in crossing the River.

Oct. 4.—Came to the mouth of the 7 mile streams, and encamp'd on a point of land.

Oct. 5.—Came to the falls called Carrytuck, otherwise Devil's Falls. They fall about sixteen feet. The carrying place is about 8 Rods, and very difficult; the water is frozen. This is the 5th carrying place.

Oct. 6.—Carried our Batteaux across, and proceeded to the Great carrying place; went about seven miles, and came to Seven Islands on the east side of the river, the mountains appearing ahead, which looked dismal to us, and especially more so, knowing we had them to cross without a conductor.

Oct. 7.—Got on our march to the great carrying place; the land is low and rich in grass. In spring time the edge of the River seems to be overflown, and gradually as we proceed, begins to be less fertile.

Oct. 8.—Lieut. Church returned with his party, who went to reconnoitre the Place, and informed us the first carrying place to be within three and one-fourth miles and then a pond. We encamped here, and employed our men in clearing the road for carrying our boats, &c. It rained hard all Day, which hindered us much. Hitherto we had fair weather. At 3 o'clock, the remainder of our Battalion came up, but we remained here. The three companies of Riflemen were helping to clear the roads; they had killed a Moose; the skin appeared to be as large as that of an ox of 600 lbs. This animal is of the same species as the Reindeer, and might be of the same service to the inhabitants as the Reindeer is to the Laplanders and Upper Norwegians. They are so numerous that we can hardly walk 50 yards without meeting their tracks; their meat is good and refreshing. We encamped here.

Oct. 9.—Detached two Subalterns and 36 rank and file, to clear the road to the first Pond. The remainder of the men were employed in unbarreling our Pork and stringing it on poles for convenience of carriage, and carrying our Batteaux from the river to the pond. The carrying place is about 4 miles long; the weather is fair, but very fresh. Here came up two companies of the other Battalion ; this pond is full of trout, of which we caught plenty. This is the 6th carrying place.

Oct. 10.—Employed getting our men over the pond; this is one-half mile distant from the preceding one, which is the 7th carrying place.

Oct. 11.—Came to the 8th carrying place, which is about four and one-quarter Miles, and made the rivulet that runs into the Dead River, (so call'd) but undeservedly, because it runs swiftly, except where the rivulet enters the river.

Oct. 12.—Had a beautiful prospect of a high mountain that bears S. S. W. of us, about fifteen miles. This last carrying place is very difficult—sinking half leg deep carrying over our Batteaux and Provisions, the ground being wet and boggy, and to add to our difficulties, we had to wade through the whole bog. At the east side of the mountain is the Creek that runs into the Dead River.

Oct. 13.—Proceeded on our march about three miles up Dead River.

Oct. 14.—Proceeded about ten miles only, the current being so strong, and the shore so bold that our poles would not reach the bottom, and were oblig'd to pull them by the Bushes that hung over the water.

Oct. 15.—Dispatch'd two Indians and a white man to deliver some letters to a gentleman in Quebec, whose return we expected in ten or twelve days ; waited some time for a company in the rear to come up ; clean'd our arms. The mountain bears W. S. W., and the River runs N. W. by W. Thick weather, and calm, with some rain, but not very cold ; the land is good.

Oct. 16.—Fell short of Provisions and brought to half an allowance per man—waited until 9 o'clock for the Rifle companies in order to get some supply, but they not appearing, we push'd our journey. Past the ninth carrying place and came to an Indian hut where one Sataness dwell'd, both as roguish and malicious as ever existed. Proceeded about 4 miles and encamped. Col. Arnold came up in the Evening, and understanding our want of supplies, ordered four Batteaux with thirty-two men of Each company to return to the rear for some. In the morning our company had but 5 or 6 pounds of flour for 60 men.

Oct. 17.—Detached 12 Batteaux with 96 men, officers included, on the above Business.

Oct. 18.—Employed making cartouches—took an observation of the mountain, which we found to be 6 miles S. E. by E.—the river runs W. N. W., and bears more to the north; the weather is fair. We tarried until Major Meigs' division arrived.

Oct. 19.—Heavy rain until 8 o'clock; then Major Meigs and his division marched on; we expect our supply of Provisions, as the officers and men are eager to get forward.

Oct. 20.—Rain'd very hard, and our Batteaux not appearing, we pack'd up our cartouches in casks in order to be ready for an immediate embarkation, having lain by 6 Days waiting for supplies to no purpose.

Oct. 21.—A continuance of rain, and a most heavy storm. Col. Enos came up with us about 11 o'clock, in expectation of finding Col. Arnold, but on his disappointment returned, and drove up his rear. In the afternoon Capt. Williams' Sergeant came up with that company. Major Bigelow, who carried the boats, returned with only 2 barrels of flour, and the detachments returned immediately to their respective companies. Now we found ourselves in a distress'd and famish'd situation, without provisions and no hopes of getting any, until we reach'd Sartigan. Having no other view now but to proceed to Canada, (or retreat) we concluded to send back such as were not able to do Duty; the river rose 8 foot, which increased the rapidity of the current. Our encampment grew quite uncomfortable, and especially to those who had no Tents, and not being much used to the inconveniencies that a soldier is obliged to undergo, suffered exceedingly.

Oct. 22.—Myself and eight more of the men, missing our way by the freshet of the River and the overflowing of the surface, were cast into the greatest consternation, not being able to make any other way but by wading through the water, in which situation we were obliged to remain without victuals or drink until the next morning about 9 o'clock, exhausted with cold and fatigue, reached the detachment as they were beginning their march. The storm abated, the river rose 6 feet perpendicular, and ran exceeding rapid. The sun rose with a little rain, but soon grew fair, and we embark'd on board our Batteaux, and after going about 6 miles against the current, which ran at least 5 miles an hour, came to a carrying place entirely overflowed, that our Batteaux went through the woods, without the trouble of carrying them; advanced about 50 rods and encamped. This is the 10th carrying place.

Oct. 23.—Proceeded a little further and came to a carrying place, which is the eleventh. At six o'clock proceeded against the freshet, being altogether as high as before, which made us repent of our Delays; went about 2 miles and cross'd another carrying place, and half a mile further cross'd again; went about 7 miles and came to another, by which we expect to be within 6 miles of the second great carrying place, and encamp'd. It is to be observed here that by ye freshet overflowing, our salt was wash'd out of the Boats, and had no more to supply our want.*

Oct. 24.—Had intelligence of its being twenty-five miles to the great carrying place where the height of land is, and in the meantime destitute of provisions, for the two Barrels we brought gave two pounds Each man, and we had only [a] half pint left to deliver out; besides, the continual snow aggravated us more, and left [us] in a situation not to be described.

Oct. 25.—We staid for Col. Greene to consult about our situation, and what to do for provisions; however we trusted in the Almighty, and hoped he would prove propitious towards us; for the present we had no hopes, unless some Glimpses from the part of the French, which at any rate could not be much. We sent back in three Batteaux, forty-eight sick men, and one subaltern; the river is narrow and of

---

**Oct.* 23. "Encamped this evening at a carrying place, fifteen perches across. Here a council was held, in which it was resolved that a captain with fifty men should march, with all despatch, by land, to Chandiere pond, and that the sick of my division and Captain Morgan's should return to Cambridge. At this place the stream is very rapid, in passing which five or six battoes filled and overset, by which we lost several barrels of provisions, a number of guns, some clothes and cash."—*Meigs' Journal.*

course rapid, Besides bad walking by land; the men are much disheartened and Eagerly wish to return—however, I am certain if their Bellies were full, they would be willing eno' to advance. Whether or no, necessity obliges [us] to proceed at present. Col. Arnold has sent with Capt. Hanchet a party of 60 men, to purchase provisions of the French, if possible. In the afternoon, went about three miles and encamped, waiting for our boats. Here Col. Greene, Capt. Topham and myself staid, by desire of Col. Enos, to hold a council of war, in which it was resolved that Col. Enos should not return back. His party, who were 6 in number, and by one inferior to ours, and observed with regret that we voted for proceeding; on which they held a council of war amongst themselves, of which were the Capts. McCobb, Williams and Scott, and unanimously declar'd that they would return, and not rush into such imminent danger; to which we replied, if thus determined to grant us some supply, which they promis'd, if we could get a boat from Mr. Copelin, tho' with ye utmost reluctance.

Mr. Ogden, a volunteer under Colonel Greene, and myself, took the Boat, in which we ran rapidly down with the current, where we expected to receive from the returning party, four barrels of flour and two of Pork, according to promise. But we were utterly deceived, and only received two Barrels of flour, notwithstanding all our entreaties, and that few only through the humanity of Capt. Williams. Col. Enos Declared to us [that] he was willing to go and take his boat in which there was some provisions, and share the same fate with us, But was obliged to tarry thro' the means of his Effeminate officers, who rather pass their time in sippling than turn it to the profit and advantage of their country, who stood in need of their assistance. Capt. Williams stept'd towards me, and wish'd me success, But in the meantime told me he never expected to see me, or any of us, he was so conscious of the imminent Danger we were to go through; in meantime Col. Enos advanced, with tears in his Eyes, wishing me and mine success, and took, as he then suppos'd and absolutely thought, his last farewell of me, demonstrating to me that it was with the utmost reluctance he remain'd behind, tho' being certain he never would escape the attempt.* I took the little flour, bemoaning our sad fate, and cursing the ill-heart'd minds of the timorous party I left behind, and working, together with Mr. Ogden and myself, up against a most rapid stream for a mile and a half, where, after inconceivable difficulties, I reach'd and met some of our boats coming to me and take the flour they suppos'd I had in theirs; but to their great surprise, they found but the little I mention'd just now. However, it is surprising that the party returning, professing christianity, should prove so ill-disposed toward their fellow-brethren and soldiers, in the situation we were in, and especially when we observe our numerous wants, and the same time they overflowing in abundance of all sorts, and far more than what was necessary for their return. But not the least, when again considering the temerity and effeminency of 'em not willing to pursue the eager desires of their Colonel, nor suffer the same fate, nor willingly assist their courageous countrymen in the plausible cause of their common Country. In the meantime, Mr. Ogden† and myself were oblig'd to keep the course towards the river, in sight of our boats, and lay that [night] disagreeably in the snow, without the least to cover or screen us from the inclemency of the Weather, until next morning.

About nine o'clock we overtook our troops, who were just ready to march forward—even had not the satisfaction

---

*"Enos, either through a false construction of the order, or willful disobedience, returned to Cambridge with his whole division. His appearance excited the greatest indignation in the Continental camp, and Enos was looked upon as a traitor for thus deserting his companions and endangering the whole expedition. He was tried by a court-martial, and it being proved that he was short of provisions, and that none could be procured in the wilderness, he was acquitted. He was never restored in public estimation, however, and soon afterward left the army."—*Lossing's Field Book of the Revolution*, vol. I, p. 192. The statement above made by Capt. Thayer would seem to justify the acquittal of Colonel Enos, and to remove, in part, the opprobrium with which historical writers have clothed his memory.

† This was MATTHIAS OGDEN, who joined the army at Cambridge, and accompanied Arnold through the wilderness. He was wounded at the assault upon Quebec. On his return from this expedition he was appointed to the command of a regiment, which position he held until the termination of the war. On the occurrence of peace, he was honored by Congress with a commission of Brigadier General in the army of the United States. General Ogden was distinguished for his liberality and philanthropy. He died at Elizabethtown, N. J., in the year 1791.

or conveniency to build ourselves, as we usually had done, a Bush hut to pass the tedious night in.

Oct. 26.—Proceeded over three carrying places, two of them small, and the third half a mile, running through a pond one-quarter of a mile, and a carrying place as much more; came to another pond and Encamped.

Oct. 27.—This Day after a cold and frosty night, went over this pond and came to another carrying place. This is the 20th carrying-place, being three-fonrths of a mile, and came to another pond and encamp'd.

Oct. 28.—Past the twenty-first carrying place, and came to another small pond, to a carrying place, and then to a pond, to a carrying place, and then to a pond, and then came to a height of land to another carrying place of four miles and a quarter.* It is to be observed here, with such horror, that the most ferocious and unnatural hearts must shudder at, when knowing the dismal situation of courageous men, solely bent to extirpate the tyranny with which the country was influenced, taking up some raw-hides, that lay for several Days in the bottom of their boats, intended for to make them shoes or moccasins of in case of necessity, which they did not then look into so much as they did their own preservation, and chopping them to pieces, singeing first the hair, afterwards boiling them and living on the juice or liquid that they soak'd from it for a considerable time.† After such sufferings they came to a small rivulet which leads into the great Ammeguntick Lake, otherwise Shadeur Pond, fourteen miles in length and six Broad. Here our division left all the Batteaux But one to carry the sick, if any; at four o'clock,

**Oct. 28th.* "In the morning crossed the heights to Chandiere river. Made division of our provisions and ammunition, and marched back upon the height and encamped. Here I delivered the following sums of money to the following persons: To Col. Greene, 500 dollars, to Major Bigelow, 501 do., and paid to Mr. Gatchel 44 dollars; paid to Mr. Berry £4, 5s. lawful money."—*Meigs' Journal.* Nehemiah Gatchel and John Horne were employed as guides.

†"They washed their moose-skin moccasins in the river, scraping away the dirt and sand with great care. These were brought to the kettle and boiled a considerable time, under the vague but consolatory hope that a mucilage would take place. The poor fellows chewed the leather, but it was leather still. They had not received food for the last forty-eight hours. Disconsolate and weary we passed the night."—*Henry's Narrative.*

an Express came from Col. Arnold, with intelligence that the French were ready to receive us, and that they would supply us with Provisions. Glad tidings to People that are brought to one pint of flour to Each man, and no more to depend upon. An Express pass'd us, going to His Excellency Genl. Washington. A pilot was sent to lead us through the woods; two companies of musketry are gone forward, but the three companies of Riflemen staid with us. This is the twenty-fourth carrying place. Here we divided our remaining flour Equally in 10 companies between the officers and soldiers, the quantity amounting to seven Pints Each man, for 7 Days, (expecting to meet the Inhabitants at that time) which we divided thus daily for our support: In the morning a gill for breakfast, half a pint for Dinner, and the remaining Gill for supper, which we mix'd up with clear water, having no salt, and stirring it up together, laid it on the coals to heat a little, after which we nibbled it along our journey, without making any halt;* walk'd about three miles and then encamp'd.

Oct. 29.—We march'd in the front; the travelling is very bad, so that we sunk half leg deep every step, but our Pilot says it is better ahead. We lost one man belonging to Capt. Topham's company who must have inevitably perish'd, to wit: Samuel Nichols. We find now that the Pilot knows no more the way than the most ignorant of ourselves; we travelled about five miles and encamped.† This night we had the good fortune to kill a partridge, of which we made good soup and some supper.

---

* "The breakfast and supper were boil'd much like starch; ye dinner was somewhat bak'd on the coals."

† "Early this morning set out for the head of Chaudiere river. This day we suffered greatly by our bateaux passing by us, for we had to wade waist high through swamps and rivers and breaking ice before us. Here we wandered round all day, and came at night to the same place we left in the morning, where we found a small dry spot, where we made a fire, and we were obliged to stand up all night in order to dry ourselves and keep from freezing."—*Ware's Journal in Gen. Reg. Vol. VI., p.* 131.

Joseph Ware, author of this journal, was the son of Josiah and Dorothy Dewen Ware, of Wrentham, Mass. He was born October 15, 1753, and married Esther Smith, of Needham. He was a farmer, and followed that occupation till the commencement of the Revolution, when he entered the army; served through the war; was at the battles of Concord and Ticonderoga; acted as orderly sergeant and recruiting officer. He died Nov. 12, 1805.—*Gen. Reg. Vol. VI., p.* 148.

Oct. 30—Proceeded through a swamp above 6 miles, which was pane glass thick frozen, besides the mud being half leg deep; got into an alder swamp; steering southerly, reach'd a small River which we forded, the water being so high that a middle sized man would be arm pit deep in it; very cold and about 8 Rods wide, from whence we proceeded to a great eminence and shaped our course N. ½ W. towards another River, being obliged to cross it on a narrow log. Many of the men unfortunately fell in. Now, verily, I began to feel concern'd about the abated situation of the men, having no more than a small share of allowance for 4 Days, in the midst of a frightful wilderness, habit'd by ferocious animals of all sorts, without the least sign of human trace. At ½ after 4, after a journey of 13 miles and bad traveling, reached a beautiful grove of birch woods, and about 2½ miles further, discovered to our great satisfaction the tracks of the foremost party, which rejoiced our men so much, that they shuddered at the thoughts of the long and painful March which they sustained with becoming courage, though famished and under the greatest inconveniences. Here we encamped at the end of the grove.

Oct. 31.—Proceeded 6 miles and came in sight of our Boats that were wrecked—March'd 6 miles further, But did not come up with Col. Arnold as we expected. A man was drowned here by the over-setting of the Boat.†

Nov. 1. Proceeded on our march; The people are very weak and begin to lack in the rear, being so much reduced with hunger and cold. Capt. Topham and myself being behind spurring on the men as well as we could, tho' the orders were

†"Pushed on for Chaudiere with all speed, in hopes of overtaking our bateaux in order to get some flour, for ours was all expended; but, to our great grief and sorrow, our bateaux were stove and the flour was lost, and the men barely escaped with their lives; now we were in a miserable situation, not a mouthful of provisions, and by account 70 miles from inhabitants, and we had a wilderness, barren and destitute of any sustenance to go through, where we expected to suffer hunger, cold and fatigue Here the captain with the ablest men pushed forward, in order to get provisions to send back for the sick."—*Ware's Journal.* "Henry says of the Chaudiere, "that for 60 or 70 miles it is a continual rapid, without any apparent gap or passage, even for a canoe. Every boat we put in the river was stove in, one part or other of it. Capt. Morgan lost all his boats, and the life of a much valued soldier.'"—*Note on Ware's Journal, Gen. Reg. VI, p.* 142. This man was named George Innis.—*Melvin.*

for every man to do for himself as well as he could. We observed at a little distance a Sergeant and 10 or 12 men round a fire, towards whom we made up, and saw with astonishment that they were devouring a Dog between them, and eating paunch, Guts and skin, part of which they generously offered us, but did not accept of it, thinking that they were more in the want of it than what we were at that time.* We pushed on and encamp'd 12 miles further, being at that period in the distressed situation the remainder were in, and after marching 2 Days and two nights without the least nourishment, traveling on the shore side, discover'd about 12 o'clock the 3d Day some men and horses and cattle making towards us, at which sight Capt. Topham and myself shed tears of joy, in our happy delivery from the grasping hand of Death. The Driver was sent towards us by Col. Arnold, in order to kill them for our support. He desir'd us stop in order that he might kill one for us, but we desir'd him proceed and not stop until about nightfall, and gather together all the men he could find, and kill one

*Nov. 1. "This day I passed a number of soldiers who had no provisions, and some that were sick, and not in my power to help or relieve them, except to encourage them."—*Meigs.*

"This morning started very early and hungry, and little satisfied with our night's rest. Travelled all day very briskly, and at night encamped in a miserable situation. Here we killed a dog, and we made a very great feast without either bread or salt, we having been 4 or 5 days without any provisions, and we went to sleep that night a little better satisfied. Our distress was so great that dollars were offered for bits of bread as big as the palm of one's hand."—*Ware's Journal.*

Judge John Joseph Henry, of Pennsylvania, was a private in Smith's company of riflemen, and in 1812 his account of the hardships and sufferings of the Expedition against Quebec was published. Under date Nov. 2, he says, "Came up with some of Thayer's and Topham's men. Coming to their fire, they gave me a cup of their broth. A table-spoonful was all that was tasted. It had a greenish hue, and was said to be that of a bear. This was instantly known to be untrue, from the taste and smell. It was that of a dog. He was a large, black Newfoundland dog, and very fat."—[Note to *Ware's Journal.*] The aforenamed dog belonged to Captain Dearborn, and though a great favorite, was given up and killed to appease the cravings of hunger. "They ate every part of him, not excepting his entrails; and after finishing their meal, they collected the bones and carried them to be pounded up, and to make broth for another meal. There was but one other dog with the detachment. It was small, and had been privately killed and eaten. Old Moose-hide breeches were boiled, and then broiled on the coals and eaten. A barber's powder bag made a soup in the course of the last three or four days before we reached the first settlements in Canada. Many men died of fatigue and hunger frequently four or five minutes after making their last effort and sitting down."—*Letter from Gen. Dearborn in Allen's Biog. Dic.*

creature for them to feed on. He inform'd us of killing one about 9 miles further for Col. Greene and the men with him, to whom we repli'd we would suffer contentedly thus far as we had done for the 2 foregoing Days, and expect'd to get something from the foregoing party whom we met about 4 o'clock, devouring with avidity a calf that was between 3 and 4 months gone, and that was taken from the cow that was kill'd a little further [on] of which we fortunately got some, and satisfied with eagerness our drooping stomachs;* after which we sat out and pass'd three pair of Falls, went one mile and Encamp'd. Came to an Indian's hut, and being hungry we call'd for victuals; had none but some few Potatoes, for 8 of which he charged us 2 pistareens.†

Nov. 4. Proceeded and came to a River which we forded, and got over without any accidents, Save only myself, when stepping from the last stone to the land, accidentally slipp'd and fell on the broad of my back, on which occasion I suffer'd exceedingly, having my clothes frozen to my back, and a march of 5 miles before I could get to any house to warm myself, which

---

*"*Nov. 2d.* This morning when we arose many of us were so weak that we could hardly stand, and we staggered about like drunken men. However, we made shift to get our packs on, and marched off, hoping to see some inhabitants this night. A small stick across the road was sufficient to bring the stoutest to the ground. In the evening we came in sight of the cattle coming up the river side, which were sent by Col. Arnold, who got in two days before. It was the joyfullest that I ever beheld, and some could not refrain from crying for joy. We were told by the men who came with the cattle that we were yet twenty miles from the nearest inhabitants. Here we killed a creature, and we had some coarse flour served out, straws in it an inch long. Here we made a noble feast, and some of the men were so hungry, before the creature was dead, the hide and flesh were on the fire broiling."—*Ware's Journal.*

"We proceeded till towards mid-day, the pale and meagre looks of my companions, tottering on their feeble limbs, corresponding with my own. Slipshod and tired, I sat down on the end of a log, against which the fire was built, absolutely fainting with hunger and fatigue."—*Henry.*

"Our greatest luxuries now consisted in a little water, stiffened with flour, in imitation of shoemakers' paste, which was christened with the name of Lillipu. Several had been entirely destitute of either meat or bread for many days."—*Senter's Journal.*

†"At this period several died, and many sickened by excessive indulgence following so suddenly in their previous famine. At this place the army was joined by an Indian named Natanis, and his brother Sabatis, and seventeen other Indians, who proceeded with them. Natanis had been represented to Arnold as a spy, and orders

however happen'd to be below the falls, where we got a little repast and paid very dear for it.*

Nov. 5.—Proceeded, and reach'd another house, where provisions were procured for the troops. We bought fowls [and] refresh'd ourselves. The people were civil, but mighty extravagant with what they have to sell.†

Nov. 6.—Being in great want of spirits, we happen'd on [a] man that lived with the indians whom we ask'd if he could procure us any, to which he answer'd yes, and got 10 of us 1 gallon of very Bad New England Rum, for which we were obliged to pay 10 pistareens.

Nov. 7.—Col. Greene, being one of 10, order'd Capt. Topham and myself to remain there 3 Days, in order to bring up the men in the rear, and push off from thence to St. Mary's; again from thence I was sent back to Sartigan by Col. Arnold, in order to hire Boats to bring up the invalids. We were well treated. The troops were provided for. Even the minister was generous eno' to let us have all he could spare. This place is well settled, and is good land all to the back mountains, which are somewhat poor.

Nov. 8.—Major Meigs met me at St. Marys with the 96 invalids, in order to purchase canoes to help them off, which we perform'd, and bought 20. Then Major Meigs left me, whom I never saw since,‡ and had to carry them 30 miles on

---

had been given to take him, dead or alive. They had now reason to consider him a friend. He was wounded in the attack on Quebec, and taken prisoner, but soon released. This is said to be the first employment of the Indians against the English in the Revolution."—*Note on Ware's Journal, Gen. Reg. Vol. VI., p.* 143. [See Appendix F.]

*"*Nov.* 4. In the morning continued our march. At 11 o'clock arrived at a French house, and was hospitably used. This is the first house I saw for 31 days, having been that time in a rough, barren, uninhabited wilderness, where we never saw human being, except our own men. Immediately after our arrival we were supplied with fresh beef, fowls, butter, pheasants and vegetables. This settlement is called Sertigan. It lies 25 leagues from Quebec."—*Meigs.*

†*Nov.* 5. "Continued our march down the river. The people very hospitable, provisions plenty but very dear, milk one shilling sterling per quart, and bread a shilling per loaf, weighing no more than 3 pounds. Came this day twelve miles."—*Ware's Journal.*

‡Meaning during the march.

our Backs, 4* men under each canoe to Point Levi, going 12 miles without meeting an house, then 15 more, and staid at St. Mary's Parish at a house near the Chapel of the same name. There we dined, and set out again for Point Levi, where we arrived about 8 o'clock. There met Col. Arnold and our volunteers all in good spirits.

Nov. 9.—This Day the Hunter, Sloop of War, sent her Boat on shore for some oars. We saw them and fir'd on them. They put off in confusion, and Mr. McKenzie, a Midshipman, who was taken and brought to Head Quarters, tried to swim off, but an Indian went in after him and brought him out. He strictly adher'd to the old doctrine of War, viz., not to discover their weakness. He is but a youth of about 15 years of age, a genteel well behaved young lad.

Nov. 10.—Remain'd, getting some Provisions, &c. We were obliged to purchase some Canoes to cross the St. Lawrence, because the enemy having timely notice of our approaching, order'd them to be destroy'd or taken away, in order to obstruct our proceedings, on which occasion Capt. Topham and Company was order'd, if possible, to secure them from the Enemy and procure some others for convenience. The Enemy had then a Sloop of War in the River, the property of Simeon Pease, of Rhode Island, and of James Frost, of the same place, who commanded her.

Nov. 11.—Capt. Hanchet took 6 smiths to make spears, Canoes, and hooks for Ladders. Lieut. Savage with a number of carpenters, went and made Ladders for scaling ye Walls of Quebec.

Nov. 12.—Capt. Hanchet returned. The same night a council of war was held, whether we were to attack or not after crossing, being carried in the negative, to the mortification of the opposite party, being informed of they having no cannon mounted, cartridges made, and even the Gates of the City open. Col. Greene, Arnold & the Rhode Island, with some other officers, were for the attack.

Nov. 13.—Continued making Ladders; receiv'd some favorable accounts from Gen. Montgomery. In the afternoon a

*16 remaining men not able to do duty.

council of War was held, wherein it was resolved to cross the River at night, which Capt. Topham and I done, but could not then bring the whole party over; however We brought the remainder over the second attempt, tho' mighty difficult on account of the Enemy lying await of us in the River.* The Hunter's Boat rowing down was hail'd by Col. Arnold, myself and 4 more, But on her not coming too, we fir'd at her, and perceived by ye screaming and dismal lamentations of the crew that there were some of them kill'd or wounded.

Nov. 14.—A boat came to Wolfe's Cove with a Carpenter & 4 men who were taken by Lieut. Webb. They were unarm'd, and bound up the River for some timber belonging to Government that lay in the Cove. They were carried to Head Quarters. One of them was a Swiss, of whom we got some intelligence; the others were Canadians. The Enemies sallied out and surpris'd one of our sentries, whereon we immediately turn'd out our men and march'd within 80 Rods of the walls, giving 3 Huzzas, and marching in such a manner that they could not discover our numbers. They fir'd some Cannon at us, But to no Effect.

Nov. 15.—This Day busy in getting our men in order and regulating Guards and other Duties. The French seem for the most part in our favor. There are some lurking about our Camp whom we suspect, But don't like to take them for fear of aggravating the minds of the People. Last night the English troops set Fire to some part of St. John's.†

---

*"Nov. 13. In the evening crossed St. Lawrence at the mill above Point Levi, and landed at Wolfe's Cove. I went back twice to fetch over the people, and staid till day. The town was alarmed by our Colonel firing at a boat in the river. We went to Major CALDWELL's house, about two miles from the city, where we were quartered; a whole company having only one small room."—*Melvin.* "We began to embark our men on board 35 canoes, and at 4 o'clock in the morning we got over and landed about 500 men, entirely undiscovered, although two men-of-war were stationed to prevent us."—*Meigs.*

†"On the 15th one of Morgan's lieutenants, with a party, reconnoitered the walls. Henry states that Arnold had only 350 effective men. Lt. Gov. Caldwell's well furnished farm house in the suburbs was occupied by the troops. Arnold formed his line without musket range in front of the walls, and kept them in position, while a thirty-six pounder of the enemy's opened upon them, and which they answered by huzzas. Henry relates that this caused much dissatisfaction in those who thought the conduct of Arnold sprung from a vain desire to parade his power

Nov. 16.—We march'd our men in order to take some live stock belonging to Government. We post'd near St. John's, But finding none, except a few Yearlings and an old Cow, we left a strong guard to cut off the communication with the City and returned.

Nov. 17.—Relieved guards and took two Gentlemen who were Capt's of the Militia in Quebec. They had been out to see what Interest they could make in the country. This Morning an Express arrived from Brig. Gen. Montgomery with some agreeable news.

Nov. 18.—This Day being relieving guards at the nunnery, Sergt. Dixon had his leg shot off by a 12 pounder, and after having it cut off, he expired in the agonies he partly went through.*

Nov. 19.—Relieved guards as usual; then, by desire of Col. Arnold, I went and got 4 Boats along the shore, after which I cross'd the river in order to bring Back some invalids that were left behind; in the meantime they holding a council of war, [it] was resolved without my knowledge, as being then on the other side, to decamp, having understood that the Enemy was inform'd of their situation, which on my return I found them to my

---

before those who had formerly contemned him as a "horse jockey,"—for Arnold had in previous years traded with the inhabitants, in horses. This parade gave Henry "a contemptible opinion of Arnold." Gordon, the historian, applauds the manœuvre. Anwell, the British historian, says their commander killed several. Henry says, all the blood spilt that day flowed from Gov. Caldwell's fattened cattle."—*Note on Ware's Journal, Gen. Reg. Vol. VI., p.* 143.

"*Nov.* 15. The commanding officer this day sent into the town a flag, concluding that the firing on our flag yesterday was through mistake; but he was treated in the same manner as yesterday, on which he returned."—*Meigs.*

*This was the first blood shed before Quebec. The casualty occurred on the 16th. Sergeant DIXON was from West Hanover, Dauphin Co., Pennsylvania, where he possessed a good estate. He held his warrant in one of the rifle companies, probably Smith's. After receiving the fatal shot, "he was conveyed upon a litter to the house of an English gentleman, about a mile off. An amputation took place—a tetanus followed, which, about nine o'clock of the ensuing day, ended in the dissolution of this honorable citizen and soldier. An anecdote of him is well worthy of record, showing, as it does, his patriotic character. The lady of the house where he was taken, though not approving of the principles or actions of the Americans, was nevertheless very attentive to Dixon, and presented him with a cup of tea, which he declined, saying, "No, madam, I cannot take it; it is the ruin of my country." Uttering this noble sentiment, he died, sincerely lamented by every one who had the opportunity of knowing his virtues."—*Henry.*

great surprise marching off. We hear likewise that they were to sally out upon us, with seven field Pieces, at which time there was a Frigate that sail'd up the River, which made us suspect the report to be true. About 3 o'clock in the morning set out for Point-au-Tremble.

Nov. 20.—An express arrived from Genl. Montgomery with ac'ts that Genl. Carleton quitted Montreal to go to Quebec, which he determines to hold out at all events.

Nov. 21.—Sent an Express to Genl. Montgomery; Besides sent a man over the River, to stop the men that were there.—It freezes smartly. Our men are brought to a distress'd situation, deficient of all necessaries, and obliged to hard Duty. Numbers of the men are working at moccasins, but the leather proves to be of a bad quality.

Nov. 22.—The Express we sent to Genl. Montgomery returned with letters from him. We set a guard of two Lieuts. and 40 men over a river and a Bridge between us and Quebec. A man belonging to Capt. Topham's company who was suppos'd to be starv'd to death, return'd and inform'd us that he and one Onley Hart kept together for some time, both sick and wading through the rivers. After being 6 days from the height of Land, Hart was seized by the cramp and expired shortly after. Burdeen and 5 Riflemen left him dead, and shortly after met another; then espied a horse that stray'd away from the man that brought us provisions, which they shot, and eat heartily of the flesh for 3 or 4 Days, with 7 or 8 more that came up; by which means they fortunately escaped the dismal pangs of Death, which they partly endur'd for 7 Days before, not having any sort of nourishment but Roots and black birch bark, which they boil'd and Drank. He inform'd us of a man and wife, belonging to the Battalion of Riflemen being Dead, with 12 more. But the woman return'd about 6 weeks afterwards, and left her husband in the last agonies.* When reflecting on the dismal marches

* Judge Henry speaks of two women, the wives of soldiers attached to the division of the army to which he belonged. Their names deserve preservation for the admiration of posterity. "One was the wife of Sergeant Grier, a large, virtuous and respectable woman." The other was the wife of a private soldier named Warner. Judge H. says, in reference to their march through the wet country near Megantic Lake, "Entering the ponds, and breaking the ice here and there with the

and the famish'd situation of our troops, it is wonderful how we are able to endure the hardships, with such undaunted courage and steadfastness; and were the Cambridge officers to review our men at present, they certainly would sooner prefer the Hospital for them than the field, tho' recruiting fast, and am willing to think, if once cloth'd and refresh'd a little, would be as eager as ever, tho' many having their constitutions Racked, are in such a condition as never to be capable of enduring half what they have done hitherto. This Place is called Point-au-Tremble. The church is dedicated to St. Nicholas. Two of our Volunteers began this Day their journey homeward.

Nov. 23.—Col. Arnold call'd a council of War, to choose a committee to examine into the conduct of Col. Enos and his detachment.

Nov. 24.—Had intelligence of 4 arm'd vessels beating up the River from Quebec. A Canoe and a Sergeant with 6 men were dispatch'd to Gen'l Montgomery with intelligence, who was coming to join us with the troops under his command.

Nov. 25.—The Hunter Sloop of War, in conjunction with a Brig and a Schooner, hove in sight and came too off Point-au-Tremble.

Nov. 26.—This Day the above Vessels stood up the River, in order to obstruct Gen'l Montgomery and his party from coming down. Seven or eight masters of Vessels that came from Quebec brought a proclamation of Gen'l Carleton, the purport of which was as follows: that Every man who would not take up arms and defend the city should be proclaim'd as traitors to their country, and be obliged to depart in 4 Days the district of Quebec, and have their Goods confiscated and their persons liable to the Law. The sailors were oblig'd to [do] soldier's duty on shore.

---

butts of our guns and feet, we were soon waist deep in mud and water. As is generally the case with youths, it came to my mind that a better path might be found than that of the more elderly guide. Attempting this, the water in a trice cooling my armpits, made me gladly return in the file. Now Mrs. Grier had got before me. My mind was humbled, yet astonished, at the exertions of this good woman. Her clothes more than waist high, she waded on before me to firm ground. No one, so long as she was known to us, dared to intimate a disrespectful idea of her."

Nov. 27.—Our Detachment was order'd to hold themselves in readiness to march at a moment's warning. Last [night] Lieut. Brown was detach'd on some Business and return'd this morning with 4 Cows, 4 Calves, 2 Horses, and a Calash belonging to the Enemy.

Nov. 28.—Capt. Goodrich with 2 subalterns, 4 Sergeants and 64 men, were detach'd to meet Gen. Montgomery's advanced guard with necessary stores, &c., and to watch the Vessels; also Capt. Morgan with a like number of men, to go before Quebeç to watch their motions. Capt. Callwel Burnt His own house, in order that we might not have the satisfaction to quarter in it, as we had done before, a poor malice tending to his own disadvantage.

Nov. 29.—Snows hard. Major Callwel's clerk was taken Prisoner, and confirms the foremention'd intelligence.

Nov. 30.—Continued snowing. The 3 vessels that went from Quebec came down the River again, much to our satisfaction.

Dec. 1.—Intelligence of Gen. Montgomery's sailing down the River with 5 Vessels, [which] had 15 Barrels of Powder and 2 Boxes of Lead.

Dec. 2.—This Day a Detachment was commanded to go down to Celer's, within a league of Quebec, under command of Capt. Hanchet, to carry down the Cannon, artillery, stores, and some provisions, in three Batteaux, which he abruptly refus'd, alleging the Danger of such an undertaking to be too imminent; upon which Col. Arnold sent for Capt. Topham and myself, enraged at the refusal of the Connecticut officer, swore he would arrest him, and desir'd it as a favor of one of us to perform the said command, which we eagerly accepted, and turning "*head or tail,*" it happen'd to fall to my lot, equally to my satisfaction, and vexation of Capt. Topham, who was always ready to Encounter the greatest Dangers.* I marched down

*"*Dec.* 2. In the morning I assisted in sending down our field artillery by land. The large cannon are ordered down in battoes, which, when landed, the battoes are to go to Point Levi for the scaling ladders."—*Meigs.*

"We retraced the route from Quebec. A snow had fallen during the night, and continued falling. To march on this snow was a most fatiguing business. By this time we had generally furnished ourselves with seal-skin moccasins, which are large, and according to the usage of the country, stuffed with hay or leaves, to keep

to the nunnery, went on board the vessel, and lodg'd. This Day Capt. Ogden arrived with stores of all kinds for the soldiers. Genl. Montgomery hove in sight; at 9 o'clock came into Point-au-Tremble. March'd our men to receive him at the shore. He received us politely. He is a genteel appearing man, tall and slender of make, bald on the Top of his head, resolute [word unintelligible] and mild, of an agreeable temper, and a virtuous General.

Dec. 3.—Orders were given to distribute Clothes to the soldiers. I went with the Batteaux which we loaded; the tide serving, towards the evening we cut through the ice for $\frac{1}{4}$ mile, and row'd down 18 miles in the night time, being so cold that we strove with the utmost Eagerness to Row, in order to keep ourselves from being frozen with cold until we reach'd Celer's. Besides, such a prodigious snow-storm rais'd that we separated, and could not come up with each other until I order'd some guns to be fir'd, by the flashing of which with the utmost difficulty we rejoined, and immediately making for the shore. The Batteaux being heavy and quite frozen, got on the Ground amongst Rocks, and the men being very impatient and not willing to remain there long, jump'd into the river, being up to their armpits in the water, and with the utmost difficulty reach'd the shore, from whence they brought some horses in order to enable me and the remainder to reach it with much less difficulty.*

Dec. 4.—This morning we landed our guns, &c., and tarried there 3 Days in a most disagreeable situation, until relieved the 9th Day by the York line, detaining such as pass'd, for fear of bringing intelligence to the Enemy, who were within 3 miles of us at St. Roques. This Day the detachment rec'd orders for

---

the feet dry and warm. Every step taken in the dry snow, the moccasin having no raised heel to support the position of the foot, it slipped back, and thus produced great weariness. On this march the use of the snow-shoe was very obvious, but we were destitute of that article. The evening brought up the riflemen at an extensive house in the parish of St. Foix, about three miles from Quebec. It was inhabited by tenants. We took possession of a front parlor on the left, Morgan one on the right, Hendricks a back apartment, and the soldiery in the upper parts of the house, and some warm out buildings."—*Henry*.

*"*Dec.* 3d. Major Brown arrived from Sorel. The soldiers drawing their clothing."—*Meigs*. [See Appendix G. for biographical sketches of officers.]

marching to visit Quebec once more.*

Dec. 5.—Fair, though cold weather.

" 6.—Two companies were sent to Beauport to watch the motions of the enemy. Capt's Duggen and Smith took a Vessel and 6 men loaded with Provisions and small stock, besides 382 Dollars belonging to Government.

Dec. 7 *&* 8.—Busied in regulating Guards and Quartering our men. Order'd three Companies to march forward, amongst whom was the Connecticut officer Hanchet, but abruptly refus'd, alleging his usual allegations of being too Dangerous, as being for the matter of half a mile expos'd to the Cannon of the enemy, on which denial Col. Arnold sent for Capts. Topham, Hurlbert and myself, to which we consented, and were expos'd for 3 weeks to the most imminent Danger, instances of which I will let the curious reader know some. Being one morning alarm'd by the continual firing of the Enemy on our quarters, Capt. Topham and myself rising out of Bed had several Balls fir'd through our lodgings; one particularly went through our bed, and pass'd midway between him and myself, without any hurt, and clear'd quite through the other end of our Room, to our astonishment. Brought 2 Field Pieces to Col. Arnold's Head Quarters.

Dec. 9.—Prepar'd for erecting a Battery. Drafted 100 men for fatigue, 100 to cover the Mortars, and 20 for an advanced guard.

Dec. 10.—This Day as soon as the Enemy perceiv'd our Battery, made a continual firing all day, throwing some shells, But to no Effect.

---

*"General orders for all to decamp, and I hired a Frenchman with his charriot, and proceeded to St. Foys, from thence to St. Charles, and took lodgings at Mr. Burrough's. *Dec. 5th.*—I had now orders to take possession of the General Hospital for the reception of our sick and wounded. This was an elegant building, situate upon St. Charles river, half a mile from St. Roque's gate. A chapel, nunnery, and hospital were all under one roof. This building was every way fit for the purpose, a fine spacious ward, capable of containing fifty patients, with one fire-place, stoves, &c. The number of sick was not very considerable at this time; however, they soon grew more numerous. The Hospital being in an advanced part of the army, I did not think it expedient to assume a residence therein as yet. In consequence of which I was obliged to visit it daily in open view of the enemy's walls, who seldom failed to give me a few shots every time."—*Dr. Senter's Journal.*

Dec. 12.—We fir'd a few Shots from our Battery.

" 13.—Furnish'd our men with 26 Rounds of Cartridges.

" 14.—Fir'd a Ball through our Breastwork, which kill'd two men and wounded 5.

Dec. 15.—We fir'd Briskly on the Town all Day.*

" 16.—There was a Brisk Cannonading on both sides, which obliged Col. Arnold to Quit his Quarters; had one man kill'd. A council of war being held, resolv'd to storm the Town.

Dec. 17.—A return was made of what Arms our men had.

" 18.—A General return was made for all the arms and ammunition wanting in our detachment.

Dec. 19.—Busied in delivering arms and ammunition to our men.

Dec. 20.—On the same Business.

" 21.—Nothing worth mentioning.†

" 24.—Busied in making Cartouches.‡

" 25.—Every Capt. of our Detachment had orders to march his Company to Mr. Desvin's, to be reviewed by Genl. Montgomery.

Dec. 26.—Nothing remarkable.

" 27.—Stormy weather. The men were order'd to hold themselves in readiness to storm the Town at the shortest notice. About 12 at night, the army being divided according to the plan the Gen'l had laid, the Capts. Smith, Topham, Hendrick

---

**Dec.* 15. "At the dawn of day our battery opened upon them, in which was mounted five guns, none larger than 12s. The enemy soon followed suit, and the fire and re-fire was almost incessant for several hours. In the afternoon a flag of truce attempted to go in, but was ordered back immediat ly, or be fired upon."—*Senter's Journal.*

Dec. 16. "Cannonade from both sides, not so severe as yesterday. A brave soldier by the name of Morgan received a grape shot under the lower edge of the left scapula, close to the axila, and went obliquely through both lobes of the lungs. Walked more than a mile, with the assistance of a mess-mate, into the Hospital. A superficial dressing was all that could be done, as violent henoptoi ensued; concluded his residence was not long."—*Senter's Journal.*

†"*Dec.* 22. Preparation is making, and things seem ripening fast for the assault upon the works of Quebec. The blessing of heaven attend the enterprise. This evening is celebrated as the anniversary of a happy event or circumstance in my life."—*Meigs.*

‡"*Dec.* 24. I was on a general Court-martial. Our chaplain, [Rev. Samuel Spring,] preached a sermon in the General Hospital, which is exceedingly elegant inside, and richly decorated with carvings and gilt work."—*Meigs.*

and myself were to attack the upper town under Gen. Montgomery, whilst the other party would make feint attack on the lower town, under Col. Greene. But the Darkness of the weather not answering to the General's expectations, was detained; but [he] favourably countenanc'd our undaunt'd courage, and said he was exceeding sorry to have stopp'd the career of so Brave men in the expectations they entertain'd in the ensuing occasion; but hoped a more favorable moment should shortly answer, in which he was willing to sacrifice his Life in adding by any means to the honor of his Brother soldiers and country; But then saw not only the impossibility of his most earnest desires, Bnt likewise the unhappy fate that should succeed the attempt, begging of them in the meantime not to be the least dismay'd or dishearten'd; that the few moments they had to draw back were only a true source to add more lustre and Glory to their undertakings: adding that, being then their Gen'l and common leader, if rushing into the imminent and inevitable Danger he foresaw, [he] was not only answerable to his country, but likewise to his merciful Creator, for the lives of his fellow soldiers, in rashly exposing them to ye merciless rage of their common Enemies.

Dec. 28.—Some of the soldiers took 4 men that refus'd to turn out, and led them from place to place with Halters round their necks, exposing them to the ridicule of the soldiers, as a punishment Due to their effeminate courage, who, after suffering in their fatigues to a degree of spirit not as yet known to be equal'd, timorously withdrew from the Laurels they were ready to gather.

Dec. 29.—A number of shells were thrown into the town. A file of men were sent into one Drummond's Still House to take a man that was suspect'd of giving intelligence to the Enemy, of whom one was wounded in bringing him off. Capt. Duggen took another, who carried on for some time a correspondence with the Enemy.

Dec. 30.—The Enemy kept up a smart fire all day on St. Roques, but Done little or no Damage. This Evening rec'd orders that the General determin'd to storm the city this night, ordering our men to get their arms in readiness.* It was very

*The entry here commenced on the 30th, was probably completed the next day, without prefixing the proper date.

dark, and snowed. The plan was as follows: Genl. Montgomery, with the York forces, Was to proceed around Cape Diamond and make his attack there. Col. Livingston, with a party of Canadians, to make a false attack on the same, and on St. John's Gate. An advanced party of 25 men to go to Drummond's wharf. Col. Arnold's detachment to attack the lower town in the following manner: Capt. Morgan's company in the front, with Col. Arnold and Lieut. Col. Greene; then Capt. Lamb's company with one field piece; then Capt. Dearborn's, Capt. Topham's and mine, and Ward's, Bigelow's in the centre, then Capt. Smith's, Hendricks', Goodrich's, Hubbard's, and Major Meigs' in the Rear.* We were to receive the signal by the firing of three sky-rockets to attack, but not observing them soon eno', Capt. Dearborn's company, on acct. of being Quartered over Charles' river, and the tide being high, did not come up, and march'd on without him, imagining he would soon overtake us. They fir'd briskly upon us as we pass'd the street for the space of half a mile, killing and wounding numbers of our men, of whom was Capt. Hubbard, who died shortly after in the hospital of Quebec.

The front having got lost by a prodigious snow storm, I undertook to pilot them, having measur'd the works before, and knowing the place. But coming to the Barrier, two field pieces played briskly on us that were placed there. But on their drawing them back to re-charge, Capt. Morgan and myself Quickly advanced through the Ports, seized them with 60 men rank and file, which was their main guard, and made Prisoners.†

*Capt. Lamb's company were York artillerists. Morgan's were the celebrated Virginia Rangers. Smith's and Hendricks' were from Lancaster and Cumberland counties, Pennsylvania. Henry thus describes their dress: "Each man of the three companies bore a rifle barreled gun, a tomahawk, or small axe, and a long knife, usually called a scalping knife, which served for all purposes in the woods. His under-dress, by no means in a military style, was covered by a deep ash-colored hunting-shirt, leggins, and moccasins, if the latter could be procured. It was a silly fashion of those times for riflemen to ape the manners of savages." "The Canadians who first saw these [men] emerge from the woods, said they were *vêtu en toile*—clothed in linen. The word *toile* was changed to *tole*, iron plate. By a mistake of a single word the fears of the people were greatly increased, for the news spread that the mysterious army that descended from the wilderness was clad in *sheet iron*."—*Lossing's Field Book I. p.* 195.

†See Appendix II.

Immediately afterwards, advancing towards a Picket, that lay further up the street, where there was a company of the most responsible citizens of Quebec, found their Capt. Drunk, took them likewise Prisoners, and taking their dry arms for our own use, and laying ours up in order to dry them, being wet, and advancing, by which time our whole party got into the first Barrier. We rallied our men, and strove to scale the second. Notwithstanding their utmost efforts, we got some of our ladders up, but were oblig'd to retreat, our arms being wet, and scarcely one in ten would fire; whereon some did retreat back to the first Barrier we had taken, and when we came there we found we could not retreat without exposing ourselves to the most imminent Dangers.

We had kill'd in our detachment Capt. Hendricks, Lieut. Cooper & Lieut. Humphreys, with a number of Privates, and in Genl. Montgomery's party there was kill'd the Brave and much to be lamented Genl. Montgomery,* and his aid-de-camp McPherson, Capt. Cheeseman, and some Privates. Col. Campbell then took the command, and order'd a retreat, so that the force of the Garrison came upon us. Capt. Lamb was wounded. There was no possibility of retreating, and they promising us good quarters, we surrender'd. Col. Arnold being wounded in the beginning of the action, was carried to the General Hospital. The number of us that did not retreat, amongst whom Were Col. Greene, Capt. Morgan, and a number of other officers and myself, with a number of Privates, after passing the first Barrier, having been for upwards of 4 hours victorious of the Lower town, in fact, and had about 130 prisoners in our possession, fell unhappily the victims of them that a little while before felt the same dismal fate with ourselves, which thinking were the only [ones,] But to our great surprise, on our coming into the upper town as prisoners, we found Capt. Dearborn and company, who miss'd his way and advanced to the palace gate, unfortunately, and to our astonishment, felt the same fate 4 hours before.

*" A drunken sailor returned to his gun, swearing he would not forsake it while undischarged. This fact is related from the testimony of the guard on the morning of our capture, some of those sailors being our guard. Applying the match, this single discharge deprived us of our excellent commander."—*Henry*.

It is much to be lamented the sad exit of this brave volunteer detachment, who, exposing their lives in the Common Cause of their Country, marching thro' wildernesses, sometimes the Tempest summoning all the forces of the air, and pouring itself from the angry north, now scaling the rolling mountains, Shooting with impetuosity into the yawning gulfs, struggling thro' the forest boughs frightful eno' to terrify the most savage nations. Now the inhabitants of the forest forsake their Dens; a thousand grim forms, a thousand growling monsters pace the Dessert, Death in their jaws, while stung with hunger and a thirst for blood. In this situation, we trembling with cold and famish'd nerves, we reach deserts not less terrifying than those we past. The more we advance, the fewer we are in number, for the strength of our Limbs was hardly able to support the weakness of our Body. Nay, even in this situation, some of our party who were not willing to expose themselves further, Earnestly wish'd we would return home with them. But no, we despised their temerity and effeminate courage, and proceeded for our destined place, contrary to their expectations, where at length we arrived, promising ourselves shortly the fruits of our Labor; But, alas, fell the victims of merciless misery. Let us consider what doleful recompence; instead of being regaled with the fruits of unwearied labor, we imagine our houses ransack'd, and our Villages plundered. We might behold our cities encompass'd with armies, and our fruitful fields cloth'd with desolation, or have been more frightfully shock'd at the images of slaughter instead of peace, with her imperial scale securing our goods, and the cheering olives sheltering our abodes, persecution brandishing her sword, and slavery clanking her chains. But then we suffer'd, promising ourselves after some time the agreeable hopes of victory, wishing an overthrow of the united forces of intestine treason and foreign invasion, which finally happen'd, and pours joy through the present age, and will transmit its influence to generations yet unborn. Are not all the blessings that can endear society or render life itself desirable, center'd in our present constitution? And were they all not struck at by that impious and horrid blow meditated by our friends and relatives in our Mother country, and seconded by factious spirits at home?

Who, then, can be sufficiently thankful for the gracious interposition of Providence, which has not only averted the impending ruin, but turn'd it with aggravating confusion on the authors of our troubles.

Liberty, that Dearest of names, and property, the best of Charters, gave an additional desire to extirpate the malignant root of Arbitrary power. But supposing the reverse should have befallen us, how could we expect a mitigation of their severity, or the tender mercies of a self thought injured King to have been less merciful. Besides, where should have been the encouragement to cultivate our little portion, or what pleasure could arise from an improved spot, if both the one and the other lay every moment at the mercy of lawless power. This embittering circumstance would spoil their relish, and, by rendering them a precarious, would render them a joyless acquisition. In vain might the vine spread her purple clusters, in vain be lavish of her generous juices, if tyranny, like a ravenous Harpy, should be always hovering over the bowl, and ready to snatch it from the lip of industry.

Jan. 1, 1776.--The officers that were taken with myself at Quebec, viz., Lieut. Col. Greene; Majors Bigelow and Meigs; Capts. Morgan, Goodrich, Lockwood, Oswald, Topham, Thayre, Ward, Dearborn, Lamb, Hanchet & Hubbard, who died of his wounds; Adjutant Steele, Volunteers Duncan, McGuire and Porterfield, Lieuts. Heath, O'Brian, Savage, Compston, Brown, Gisdale,* Clark, Humphrey, Webb, Slocum, Shaw, Andrews, Hutchins, Thomas & Nichols, Lieut. McDougall; Adjutant Nebegry, & Chattin, Quartermaster, were altogether imprisoned on the first of January, being a bad method to begin the new year. However, there was nothing to be done but strive to content ourselves as well as time and place afforded us.†

---

* Written *Tisdale* in the list of officers.

† "*January ye 1st*, 1776. We had a straw bed betw een two, and a blanket each man served us.—*Melvin*. Our allowance of provisions is one pound of bread, and a half pound of pork, and one gill of rice for a day, and 6 oz. of butter for a week.— 2d. In prison. This day we had a cask of porter sent us by some gentlemen of the town."—*Ware's Journal*. "Henry says that the merchants obtained General Carleton's leave to make them [the prisoners] a New Year's present. It was a large butt of porter, with a due quantity of bread and cheese. They shared more than a pint a man!"—*Note on Ware's Journal*.

Jan. 2.—Major Meigs was allow'd to go out on his parole and get our Baggage, and to return on Friday. We were visited by the officers of the Garrison.

Jan. 3.—By consent of the General, Doct. Bullen came and Innoculated 16 of us; 3 had it the natural way, of whom one Died. Again visited by the officers of the garrison.

Jan'y 4.—Major Meigs return'd with the Baggage.

" 5.—We had Liberty to visit the officers that were not innoculated, on acct. of their having it before, which made our situation more agreeable, But could not keep a regular journal any longer, the General having order'd us to be depriv'd of our Pens & ink, &c.* We were lodg'd in two separate Rooms. But on one Mr. Hutchins saying that there were a number of our men outside, in the hearing of one of the sentries, we were instantly oblig'd to lodge in one Room, which was very disagreeable, as some of us were ill, besides being 36 officers of us, and 3 boys, in a small room about 30 foot square; thus continuing, having Daily a field officer to visit us.† After Capt. Lamb return'd from the Hospital, the Barrier was alter'd further back, and we were allow'd 2 small rooms for 12 of us to sleep in, which prov'd exceeding satisfactory. Continuing in this Lamentable situation for some time, and seeing no hopes of relief, we unanimously resolv'd to make our escape if possible. Accordingly we curried the favor of one of the sentinels, who we found willing to be of our party, having inform'd us of the situation of the Garrison, the strength of our forces, and the General's name. In consequence,‡ amongst the number of officers Capt. Lockwood

---

* "*Jan.* 9. Very dark weather and snowed. Some more taken with the small pox, and we expect it will be a general disorder, for we are very thick, nasty and lousy. Our living is salt pork, biscuit, rice and butter, and a sufficiency allowed if we were not checked in our weight by one Dewey, who is appointed our quartermaster sergeant, to deal out our provision. We have not above three oz. of pork a day, and not half a pint of rice, and two biscuit a day."—*Melvin.*

† "*Feb.* 16. One of our men named Parrot, put in irons for calling one of the emigrants a tory. Our army opened a battery."—*Melvin.*

‡ Under date March "30th to 31st," Ware says, "Most of the prisoners consulted together to break out of prison, to try their best to take the town." Their plan was frustrated by noise made while cutting away ice at the cellar door, and by one of their number turning informer. Their room and packs were searched for arms and ammunition, without discovering any, and the prisoners were then put in

and myself were pitch'd upon to make our Escape. Accordingly we sounded *Joe*, (who we shall name the above sentinel,) and found him desirous to assist us as much as laid in his power. He furnish'd us with clubs apiece, and answering the countersign, we were to pass out of the chamber window, 4 stories high, by the means of our blankets tied together, expecting the signal from Joe, which was to be observed by 3 claps on the breach of his gun, and an Equal number of siffling thro' his fingers, which was partly done for three succeeding nights, but unfortunately hinder'd by the means of the patrols, who were continually watching, or some others not less interesting.*

Finding, with the utmost regret, that our plan was not seemingly to answer our expectations, we meditated another not less dangerous, which was as follows: By cutting off the planks which were spik'd on the Door, we could pass to the garret thro' a dormant window; from thence by the means of a ladder and a jump of about 14 foot into the yard, where we were to meet Joe arm'd with his Gun and sufficient clubs to furnish us with, and make towards the sentinels, who were 4 in number, who we intended passing by the means of the countersign that Joe had; but then on the least suspicion were resolved that they should not obstruct us, and push our way to the Sally Port, from whence we were to leap about 30 foot down into the snow, standing then about 6 foot high, and make immediately to our own men, who were not far distant. But to our mortification, all our intended hopes proved only false illusions. When thinking ourselves at liberty we were the farther from it; for on the

---

"strong irons." To carry out the enterprise of escape, Joseph Ashton, a sergeant in Capt. Lamb's company, was chosen leader, with a full compliment of subordinate officers. Henry says, "they were divided into two detachments, one to attack the guard house, the other the gate, when they were to turn the cannon upon the town. They intended to make the sally by the cellar door, and the officers had planned that the ice should be removed silently with their long knives, on the night of their rising. One of their number escaped to the army without, and gave notice to them to act in concert. By artifices they had procured a small supply of powder from the sentries, for matches, &c." [See Appendix I.] The person who gave the whole secret of the plot was an English deserter, who had joined the camp at Cambridge. His name was John Hall.

*"*March* 17. The guard set over us are old Frenchmen and boys, who are very saucy, telling us we shall be hanged; pointing their bayonets at us; threatening to shoot us for opening a window, or any such trifle."—*Melvin.*

26th of April, all things being ready for the Event, I open'd the door and went up to the Garret to make some necessary observations. I perceived that the door open'd With difficulty, and taking my knife to cut some more of the boards, to have it open with less difficulty, Mr. Lockwood standing in the gangway to notify me of any persons coming, observed the officer of the guard advancing towards us, who was Earlier inform'd of the fact, and finding the door open'd and ye planks unspiked, followed me into a separate room, enquiring my motive for acting so, and who were concerned with me; to which I replied that there were none but myself, and that my sole motive was only to go up to the garret to view the town and forces around it, as being a more convenient place than any other I knew of. He said that it was impossible for me to perform such a difficult work without the rest, or at least some of them being privy to it. To which I candidly answered, that I never work'd at it only when they were out of the way; besides, the place being so exceeding dark that they could not notice me, working Daily and leisurely at it for two months. On which confession he lock'd us all up together in one Room, and inform'd Col. McLane, the commanding officer, of it, who after a short interval return'd, accompanied by some officers and a guard; at which my Brother officers and Prisoners were greatly alarm'd, and earnestly show'd & desir'd to undergo the same fate with myself. But I told them that it was better for one to suffer than such a number, & that I was solely bent to undergo whatever was allotted me, & taking my leave of them I was committed to the care of a Capt. of the Main guard for some time, & a little after to the care of a Captain of the Provost, who treated me generously, from whence I was carried the next morning at 9 o'clock by the guard board a schooner, carrying 9 6-pounders & 36 men, & closely kept in the hold, both handcuffed & ironed, lying on a plank in the turnkling of a cable, being 2½ foot frozen, and no more room to walk in than 2½ steps, & the deck so low that I was obliged to keep myself always stoop'd, & my irons being so small that my wrists were striped & swell'd; so that after some Days sufferings, and on my continual complaining, the smith at length came, who was obliged to cut them and replace them with larger ones.* On the 30th, to my surprise, Capts. Lockwood & Hanchet were detected in inquiring of Joe some particulars concerning me & where I was, for they were ignorant of my destiny; & on Joe's discovering everything from the very beginning until then, to the officer, he was sent to England on board of a ship, & the Capts. to accompany me, where we remain'd in the most lamentable situation until the 6th of May, in the afternoon, being the Day the fleet arrived from England; from whence we were sent back to our former Prison, where we found our Brother officers in the same Situation as we left them.

May 6.—Last night we heard some guns fired down the River, and in the morning saw a frigate coming up to Point Levi, keeping a constant firing, on which the Garrison fir'd into the river, to let them know they were in possession of the place, on which she came up and saluted the Garrison. About 10 o'clock a 50 Gun ship came up, Capt. Douglass commander, & saluted; likewise a 14 Gun sloop with some troops, who, with those already in the fort, sallied out, and our men retreated with such precipitation that they left their cannon, stores, ammunition, and even the General's Coat and Dinner, behind.† In the Evening, a small sloop went down the River with Pilots for the fleet that is expected. A frigate and a sloop of war went up the River to take some Vessels from our People. They took a sloop & a Brig which our people had scuttled and left. Lieut. McDougal & three men were taken in a schooner with 13 Barrels of Powder.

May 7.—Brigade Major LeMatre was sent by Genl. Carleton to let us know that he intended henceforth to use us with as much humanity as lay in his power, and hop'd we would make Good use of it. We had again the Liberty to walk in the

*"*April* 14.—Major McKenzie came in and took Capt. Morgan's company out of irons."—*Melvin.*

†"This morning 3 ships came in with a re-inforcement of about one thousand men. All the bells in the town rang for joy most of the day. Then all the forces in the town marched out on Abraham's Plains to have a battle with our people, but they retreated as fast as possible, and left a number of sick in the hospital. Likewise some of their cannon and ammunition, with a number of small arms and packs."—*Ware's Journal.*

passage, of which we had been debarred for some time. We were, this afternoon, Visited by Lord Petersham & Major Carleton. He is genteel, polite and humane. Caldwell was expressing himself in his sneering, customary Way, mentioning that he suffered much by our People, on which Maj. Carleton reproved him in these words: "You should not say anything disagreeable to them in their unfortunate situation. You must consider us all as Brothers." He said there were numbers of Hessians and Hanoverians coming to America.

May 8.—The remainder of the 29th Regiment and some of the Artillery arrived. We were visited by the officers, who enquired for the Troops that were taken at St. John's, &c.

May 9.—Were visited by some officers of the 29th regiment, especially a very polite gentleman, a Lieut. of Grenadiers. A small schooner came up. They have men out Daily to pick up the sick men our people left behind. They have taken a great number of papers, among which was an Orderly book. This Day was taken Lieuts. Randall & Stephen McDougal on board the schooner Mary. By the news he brings we are in hopes things are not so bad as the people of the Garrison reported. However, I think it is bad Enough.

May 10.—Two transports came up from Halifax with Provisions and part of the 47th Regiment.*

May 11.—Were visited by Col. McLane and other officers, and were allowed to walk in the garden. Major Carleton visited us, and said that there were 55000 men designed for America this summer. We desir'd him to obtain liberty for our servants to cook for us, which he promised to do.

May 12.—This day he brought us an answer that we might walk in the garden. Two transports arrived with troops.

May 13.—We are this Day indulged more than common, and allowed to go up stairs as often as we please. A Brig came too off Beauport.

---

*"*May* 10. Two riflemen were taken out of jaol; we don't know on what terms. Same day two Jersey dumpling eaters were brought in; they were found among the bushes, not having tried to make their escape, being too heavy laden with dumplings and pork, having forty pounds of pork, a knapsack full of dumplings, and a quantity of flour."—*Melvin*.

May 14.—About 9 o'clock a broad pendant was hoisted aboard the *Isis* man of war of 50 guns. Was saluted by all the Ships in the Harbor, and returned 15 Guns. On the main top-mast head was hoisted a white pendant, and a pendant on her ensign staff. The Garrison saluted with 15 guns. In the afternoon a frigate went down the River. At night an armed schooner went up the River. Major Meigs went out with Doctor Mahon to get Mr. Monroe to supply us. He has obtained the General's promise of going home on his parole. We have had fair weather, except now and then a shower. The tide has risen here from 19 to 22 feet with an easterly wind, & from 16 to 19 with a westerly. The wind in the spring blows from eastward to northward, with showers of rain. It is very common for it to rain one half hour, and suddenly clear up. They continue to lock us up every night as yet.

May 15.—This Day we were once more allowed to use our pens and Ink, having had none but a few pencils undiscovered, by which means we kept our journals. Major Meigs was call'd upon by the General, and promised to go off in a few Days to Halifax on his way home.

May 16.—This day the Hunter Sloop of war sail'd for England with dispatches, in which went passengers Capt. Hambledon & Major Caldwell & his family. We had liberty to write letters by Major Meigs, provided we wrote nothing concerning the Garrison.

May 17.—Lieut. Born carried our letters to Col. McLane to be examined. A small Sloop came up. Major Meigs had liberty to walk the town until 4 o'clock. Mr. Laveris came and informed Capt. Dearborn that he had obtained liberty for him to go home on his parole, & that he must get ready to go on board immediately. In the Evening they took their leave of us, & went on board the schooner Magdalen.

May 18.—About ten o'clock they set sail for Halifax.

" 19.—Saw a Sloop of War come down, & the Commodore came down about noon and saluted. There were a number of officers walking in the Garden, one of them not above 15 years of age. The Drummers of the 29th Regiment are Blacks, & the band wear red feathers in their hats, and look very neat.

May 20.—Doctor Mäben visited Mr. Porterfield, a sick volunteer, and told him he would endeavor to get him a parole to go home. We were allowed two small Rooms for part to lodge in, to our great satisfaction.

May 21.—General Carleton went up the River with 3 Vessels, in order if possible to drive our Army out of Canada. The ships and Garrison saluted the General at his departure. A Canadian told us that the 8th Regiment, which lay at Detroit, fort Hannicks & Swagocha, with about 500 Indians, were down within 9 miles of Montreal, to a place called Lasheen, where they had an engagement,—kill'd and wounded 150 of our men; to which report we can hardly give any credit.

May 22.—We were told by one Capt. McDougal that the Virginians laid down their arms, and that there are more in the Interest of Government than in the Interest of Liberty, which does not seem probable. We hear that Montreal is taken.

May 27.—Some ships and transports came up, and were order'd immediately for Montreal.

May 31.—Last night after 12 o'clock we heard the sentry hail 3 times & fir'd, on which occasion we looked out and saw the guard searching for the object, which we believed was no more than conceit, or rather a trap laid by some of our Enemies, that we might be more closely kept.

June .—4 ships came up, the Intent of which is, as I conceive, to offer terms of reconcilliation with the sword at the breast of the Americans. This Army consists of Britains, Irish, Hanoverians, Hessians, &c. Oh! Britain, Britain, how art thou fallen, that thou dost hire Foreigners to cut thine offspring's throats! 19 more ships came up. We were visited by some Hessian officers. 6 more ships came up in the Evening. The ships are to go up the River with the troops to give the Provincials battle.

June 5.—We hear that the Indians under the command of Capt. Foster, took a number of the Provincials prisoners, and made them promise never to take up arms against the King again, and that they should [send] back as many of the King's troops as there is of them in the way of exchange. They kept several officers as hostages. They told them, with hatchet at their heads, that they would suffer immediate Death if they [did] not comply with their promise. They bored their Ears, that they might know them again.

June 6.—We learn that his Excellency proposed to our men to swear allegiance to the king, and that he would send them home. They are almost naked, and very Lousy & full of the scurvy, many of them unable to Walk, being lame in their knees lying so long in an unwholesome place; all salt provisions, the weather very cold and but little or no fire, & 30 in a Room about 12 foot square. But were before much closer confined, being about 6 months imprison'd, without money or friends to assist them, But enemies continually threatening, scoffing and abusing them, calling them Rebels, cut-throats, traitors, robbers, murderers, and deluded fools. This was Major Caldwell's language & some others to them. They have not sworn yet, and what they intend doing is uncertain. By what I can learn, they must either swear or die, if they remain much longer in this Dungeon.*

---

*"*June 5.* This day General Carlton with a number of his officers came to see us, and enquired of us whether we had fared as well as they promised us we should when we were taken. We told him we fared very well. He said he did not take us as enemies, & likewise said if he could rely upon our honors, he would send us to New England, if we would be quiet and peaceable, and not take up arms any more.

"*June ye 6th, A. D.* 1776. A copy of an answer sent to Gen'l Carlton.

MAY IT PLEASE YOUR EXCELLENCY:

We, the prisoners in His Majesty's goals, return your Excellency our most happy and unfeigned thanks for your clemency and goodness to us whilst in imprisonment. Being sensible of your humanity, we give your Excellency thanks for your offer made us yesterday, and having a desire to return to our friends and families again, we promise not to take up arms against His Majesty, but remain peaceable and quiet in our respective places of abode, and we further assure your Excellency that you may depend on our fidelity.

So we remain your Excellency's humble servants,
Signed in behalf of the prisoners.

August 4th. The General sent for all the prisoners to come in who were out in the country at work, that were minded to go home.

5th. This day ninety-five prisoners embarked on board the ship.

7th. This day the men all in good spirits, and embarked on board the ships. Sixty of the prisoners on board the Mermaid.

11th. This morning the signal was given for sailing. Weighed anchor and went down about one mile. At night weighed anchor and went down the river thirteen miles. The weather cold and stormy.

Sept. 6th. We were informed by the shipmen, according to reckoning, that we were in the latitude of Philadelphia, Latitude 39° North."—*Ware's Journal.*

June 7.—We addressed the General with the following Petition, in order that he might grant us a Parole to go home, But rec'd no answer as yet.

MAY IT PLEASE YOUR EXCELLENCY:

Impressed with a deep sense of your Excellency's humanity and benevolence, & urged by the peculiarity of our present disagreeable situation, being destitute of both friends & money, we beg leave that your Excellency will condescend to take our case into consideration, & grant us relief by permitting us to return to our respective homes on our Parole, which we shall ever deem sacred, assuring your Excellency that we shall make it a point to surrender ourselves to any of His Majesty's Officers, when and where your Excellency may think proper to direct. Being likewise sensibly touched with the state of our men who remain prisoners at present, we take the liberty to recommend them to your Excellency's consideration, earnestly soliciting that some measures may be taken for their relief; & we should be extremely happy if they could possibly return to their families, many of whom must be reduced to the greatest distress. Your Excellency's compliance will be esteem'd a singular favor, & ever greatly acknowledged by

Your Excellency's Most obedient & very

Humble servants.

[This petition is also contained in a small memorandum book kept by Captain Thayer, and is in his hand writing. Attached to it are the following names: The heading of the list is, "*Officers taken December* 31, 1775." The names are inserted here, though without positive evidence that they constituted a part of the petition. E. M. S.]

Names.	*Col. or Provinces.*	*Town or County.*	*Commissions.*
Christopher Greene,	Rhode Island,	Warwick,	Lieut. Colonel.
Timothy Bigelow,	Massachusetts,	Worcester,	Major.
Return Jonath'n Meigs,	Connecticut,	Middleton,	Major.
Daniel Morgan,	Virginia,	Frederick Co.,	Captain.
Will'm Goodrich,	Massachusetts,	G't Barrington,	Captain.
Samuel Lockwood,	Connecticut,	Greenwich,	Capt.
Eleazer Oswald,	do.	New Haven,	Capt. Volunteer.
John Topham,	Rhode Island,	Newport,	Capt.

Names.	*Col. or Provinces.*	*Town or County.*	*Commissions.*
Simeon Thayre,	Rhode Island,	Providence,	Capt.
Samuel Ward,	do.	Westerly,	Capt.
Jonas Hubbard,	Massachusetts,	Worcester,	Capt., dy'd of his
Henry Dearborn,	New Hampshire,	E. Nottingham,	Capt. [wounds.
*John Lamb,	New York,	City,	Capt.
Oliver Hanchet,	Connecticut,	Suffield,	Capt.
Archibald Steele,	Pennsylvania,	Lancaster,	Adjutant & Lieut.
Matthew Duncan,	do.	Philadelphia,	Volunteer.
William Heath, [Heth,]	Virginia,	Frederick Co.,	Lieutenant.
Peter O'Brien Bruen,	do.	do.	Lieutenant.
John M'Guire,	do.	do.	Volunteer.
Charles Porterfield,	do.	do.	Volunteer.
Abijah Savage,	Connecticut,	Middleton,	Lieutenant.
John Compston,	Massachusetts,	Sawco,	Lieut.
Samuel Brown,	do.	Acton,	Lieut.
James Tisdale,	do.	Medfield,	Lieut.
John Clark,	do.	Hadley,	Lieut.
Will'm Humphrey,	Rhode Island,	Providence,	Lieut.
James Webb,	do.	Newport,	Lieut.
Edward Slocum;	do.	Tiverton,	Lieut.
Sylvanus Shaw,	do.	Newport,	Lieut.
Ammi Andrews,	New Hampshire,	Hillsborough,	Lieut.
Nath'l Hutchins,	do.	Dunbarton,	Lieut.
Joseph Thomas,	do.	Deerfield,	Lieut.
Francis Nichols,	Pennsylvania,	Cumberl'nd Co.	Lieut.
Randolph S. M'Dougal,	New York,	City,	Lieut. May 7, 1776.
Christian Phebeger,	Denm'rk kingd'm	City Cop'hagen	Adjutant.
Benjamin Chatlin,	Connecticut,	Wethersfield,	Quartermaster.

The answer to the above petition was, that he could not grant it with propriety. We hear that the Provincials have taken the 8th Regiment, and that there are great divisions in Great Britain concerning American affairs. We wrote a second petition to the General, but what will be the effect of it we cannot tell. We saw some of our men who had taken the oath; they looked very pale. We hear that a considerable number of them lost the use of their limbs. We have received an answer to our last Petition, viz: that we may go home on our parole.

June 9.—We are informed that Gen'l Washington has taken Bunker's Hill, with 1500 prisoners.

June 14.—Nothing remarkable until the 14th, when we heard that the Provincials have kill'd 50 of the Hessians, & sunk three of their ships that attempted to pass our works at Sorell, & that Philadelphia is beseiged by the King's troops.

June 16.—We hear of two skirmishes, in which a considerable number of men has been slain at or near Sorell. Gen'l Thompson and his aid-de-camp were taken.

June 19.—A shower of Hail, the Stones of which were as large as walnuts. A woman was kill'd by the Lightning.

June 23.—The Provincials have Burnt Fort Chambelee, and retreated to St. John's. It is reported they are from 300 to 7000 in number.

June 24.—The Hon. Lieut. Governor made us a present of a gall. rum. Two vessels came down the river with the prisoners taken at St. John's, Chambelee, &c.

June 26.—We hear that the 12 United Provinces declared themselves independant, & have sent to France for assistance; also that they received a great Quantity of ammunition & 6000 stand of arms from them.

June 27.—Two vessels came up & saluted, which was returned by the Commodore; we are prohibited from going to the walls of the garden, for what reasons I don't know.

July 4.—Nothing remarkable until the 4th, when we hear that Gen'l Carleton has sent for all the troops that can be spared to pass Lake Champlain. 4 Provincial Officers informed us of their being taken by the Indians, viz: that they and 4 more officers & 3 soldiers went fishing, and that they crossed the river, to go to a house to get some Beer; unfortunately were not armed, thinking themselves secure from Danger; they soon heard the boy halloo, and running out to see the occasion, they were fir'd on by 13 Indians; they tried to get off the Boat, but before they got it off they kill'd one officer and wounded another; they then ran down upon them, when two found means to escape. They took five officers alive, one of which they tomahawk'd, and scalp'd. The 2 officers took off with those that they did not kill. They tied them round the necks with their Belts, and made them run before them about a mile. They stopped and hallood for their comrades, & paraded them to show the great feats they had done; they sat out again, & night coming on, they made them lie on their backs, and tied them down, & lying on the ends of their Belts they went to Sleep. In the morning they set out again. One of the Indians Snapp'd his Gun at Wm. McFarlin, & then drew his own sword upon him;

they then stripp'd them to their Breeches, and carried them to Montreal.*

July 6.—Last night we were lock'd up in our Rooms, for what reason I don't know. This morning 6 vessels arrived. I believe loaded with provisions.

July 7.—Several officers of the Garrison came and looked round in our apartments, but said nothing to us. We were ignorant of the reason until some Sea Captains came into the Garden and told us there was a report in town that we intended to set the Seminary on fire, but they are false reports, & I don't imagine there is not one amongst us that would perform such an action.

July 8.—Different reports. Some say that the Provincials took about 5000 British Prisoners. Others say that the British have taken New York, & that the Pennsylvania & Virginia [troops] laid down their arms. But the reports are so numerous and various that we can hardly credit the least; next Evening a Sloop of war sail'd down the river.

July 12.—We hear that Major Meigs and Capt. Dearborn are exchanged by Admiral Howe.

July 17.—Nothing remarkable until the 17th, when we hear of a Skirmish take place at Point-au-faire, the Provincials seeing them in their boats, which they stove to Pieces, Killed, wounded and took 400; at 4 o'clock a Brig sail'd up the River.

July 18.—Locked up close in our rooms all night; the reason we are ignorant of.

July 19.—The Lizard Ship sail'd for New York. We understand that as soon as the General comes from Montreal we are to be sent home. He is daily expected. Moderate weather until the 22d, when accompanied with a Thunder Storm†.

July 22.—The Bland 32 Gun Ship sail'd this morning for London. A brig & sloop sailed shortly after. Genl. Carleton

---

*"*July* 5. The prisoners brought in last night inform us that the Indians scalped many of our soldiers, some of them alive; but that General Carleton, to his great honor, has refused to pay those murdering fiends for any more scalps, but will pay them the same reward for every prisoner."—*Melvin.*

†"*July* 19. The weather is so cold that the Canadians do not expect a good crop of corn. It is so cold as to wear a great coat."—*Melvin.*

arrived in town this afternoon, & was saluted with a volley of 15 Guns from the Garrison, to our great satisfaction, because our fate will be shortly determined. Nothing worth notice until the 26th but some vessels going up and down the River.

July 26.—Capt. Foy informed us of the General's countenancing our going home, & was sorry we were detained so long.

July 28.—We hear that Gen. Thompson is to go home with us.

" 29.—Genl. Carleton hearing our extreme want of money, was generous Eno' to send us £100, which we are determined to repay to some British officers, Prisoners in America, as a necessary token of gratitude.*

July 30.—Genl. Thompson came to see us, and told us Gen. Carleton desired him to call on us & let us know the terms we were to go home on.

Aug. 1.—Genl. Thompson & several other Gentlemen came and brought a copy of the Parole, which we did not like; on which he said it might perhaps be alter'd, if not we must necessarily remain here longer.

Aug. 2.—Genl. Carleton sent us word that he would leave out the words we objected to, which were, "that we should never take up arms against His Majesty." This we did not think proper to sign to.

Aug. 3.—The town Major & Mr. Murray brought our Parole, which we signed.

Aug. 4.—We hear that Genl. Washington refuses to exchange the men taken at the Cedars, & Genl. Carleton keeps 16 men who came over the Lake as a Flag.

---

*In his treatment of the American prisoners, General Carleton was humane. The incident here mentioned by Captain Thayer is honorable to his character as a generous enemy. When criticised by his officers for his leniency towards his prisoners, he replied,—"Since we have tried in vain to make them acknowledge us as brothers, let us send them away disposed to regard us as first cousins." Having been informed that many persons, suffering from wounds and various disorders, were concealed in the woods and obscure places, fearing that if they appeared openly they would be seized as prisoners and severely treated, he issued a proclamation, commanding the militia officers to search for such persons, bring them to the general hospital, and procure for them all necessary relief, at the public charge. He also invited all such persons to come forward voluntarily, and receive the assistance they needed, assuring them "that as soon as their health should be restored, they should have free liberty to return to their respective provinces." Few names that stand out in the history of the events in which he was concerned are remembered with more respect, even in the country of his foes.—*Sparks.*

Aug. 5.—Had orders to be ready at a minute's warning for embarking.

Aug. 6.—Our men were oblig'd to sign a Paper, the contents I know not. We are informed that we are to embark to-morrow at 9 o'clock.

Aug. 7.—About 9 o'clock this morning I, with some more officers and 77 of our men, embark'd on board a Ship of near 400 Tons, Joseph Lawton, master, accompanied by three other Ships.

Aug. 8.—Capt. Foy wish'd us well, and said when we met again we should be friends, this gentleman & Mr. Murry having come on board to see how we were accommodated.

Aug. 9.—Waiting for the remainder of the Prisoners to come down the River; dividing out stores to the men.

Aug. 10.—About Eleven o'clock a Brig hove in sight, & the Prisoners were put on board of us.

Aug. 11.—About 11 o'clock weighed anchor, & went below the town. The [wind] blowing hard at East, we came again to anchor.

Aug. 12.—Weigh'd anchor and proceeded on our passage; spoke with the Jno. Rogers. Saw a brig wreck'd on the east end of St. Johns. Arrived Sept. the 12 at Sandy hook, after a tedious voyage, & had the mortification to see N. York in flames, when our people Evacuated it. Landed the 20th Sept. in Elizabethtown, with 9 Rank and file, & 1 Lieutenant, (named Humphrey,) being the remainder of the number we had when I left Cambridge, being 87, officers included; [the residue] perish'd by different casualties, as dying by different diseases, such as in prison, some thro' hunger & fatigue, others running away, others listing with the British, others dying with the small pox, &c; [started from Elizabethtown,] from whence each man steer'd home to his native place; accordingly [did so] myself, where I remained until 1st of July, when I was exchanged, & took up arms again in defence of my country.

THE RHODE ISLAND PRISONER.

A Sonnet.—Page 74.

The Prison-ship,—a tomb of living men,
Living in death, and longing but to die;
Or sadder still, the Royal prison, then
The foulest spot beneath the patient sky.
Both these have proved undaunted Yankee hearts,
Yet in their sad extremity forlorn,
Kind nature solaced with her tenderest arts
Those faithful souls by wasting torture torn.
For some Rhode Island captive, as he lay,
Saw in his sleep, with eager joy elate,
The level shores of Narragansett Bay,
And the plain landscape of his native State,
While his pale, dreaming lips did softly ope,
And murmur low her flag's dear legend, "Hope."

George William Curtis.

22d June, 1865.

APPENDIX.

Note A., Page 2.

Under the head "March to Newburyport," the entries upon the Journal against the dates Sept. 13 and 14, are obviously erroneous. The night of the 13th was probably spent in Malden, on the line of march to Beverly, and the night of the 14th in Beverly, about midway between Malden and Newburyport. Joseph Ware, a member of Captain Samuel Ward's company, whose journal is frequently cited in these pages, says he encamped on the evening of the 14th in Beverly. Captain Thayer may not have commenced his journal until he reached Newburyport, and there made these entries under a lapse of memory. On arriving at Newburyport, the riflemen, under Captain Morgan, encamped in the field, near Rolfe's lane. The other troops occupied two of the rope-walks in town.

Note B., Page 2.

"*Sept.* 19.—Embarked our whole detachment, consisting of 10 companies of musketmen and 3 companies of riflemen, amounting to 1,100 men, on board 10 transports. I embarked myself on board the sloop Britannia. The fleet came to sail at 10 o'clock, A. M., and sailed out of the harbour and lay to till one o'clock, P. M., when we received orders to sail for the river Kennebeck, fifty leagues from Newburyport —received with our sailing orders the following for signals, viz.

1st signal. For speaking with the whole fleet. Ensign at maintop-masthead.

2d signal. For chasing a sail. Ensign at foretop-masthead.

3d signal. For heaving to. Lanthorn at maintop-masthead, and wo guns if head on shore, and three if off shore.

4th signal. For making sail in the night. Lanthorn at masthead, and four guns; in the day jack at foretop-masthead.

5th signal. For dispersing and every vessel making the nearest harbor. Ensign at main peak.

6th signal. For boarding any vessel. Jack at maintop-masthead, and the whole fleet drawn up in a line, as near as possible.

The wind being fair and very fresh, I was very sea-sick.

20th. In the morning we made the mouth of Kennebeck, right ahead, which we soon entered. The mouth of the river is narrow. We were hailed from the shore by a number of men under arms, which were stationed there. They were answered, that we were Continental troops, and that we wanted a pilot. They immediately sent one on board. The wind and tide favoring us, we proceeded up the river; 5 miles from the mouth lies an island called *Rousack*. Upon this island is a handsome meeting-house, and very good dwelling houses. The river to this island of very unequal width, from one mile to a quarter of a mile wide, the water deep, great tides, the shore generally rocky; ten miles from the mouth some elegant buildings, at a place called Georgetown;* twenty miles from the mouth is a very large bay called Merry-meeting Bay; 25 miles from the mouth an island, called Swan Island. Little above this island we came to anchor, opposite to Pownalborough, where is a block-house. I would mention here, that this day makes fourteen only since the orders were first given for building 200 battoes, collecting provisions for and levying 1,100 men, and marching them to this place, viz., Gardner's Town; weather fine.—*Meigs' Jour.*, pp. 8–11.

Note C., Page 3.

James McCormick, (not Jno., as written by Captain Thayer,) was tried by a court-martial at Fort Western, found guilty, and sentenced to death. The sentence was approved by Colonel Arnold, but the prisoner was respited and sent on board the transport Broad Bay, Capt. Clarkson, to Capt. Moses Nowell, of Newburyport, who was ordered to convey him under a proper guard to General Washington at head-quarters in Cambridge, for his final decision upon the case. McCormick denied the crime until he was brought to the place of execution, when he confessed it. He was a resident of North Yarmouth, Mass., and was

*"At this place, in Georgetown, opposite Phipsburg, it is believed the late Gov. Sullivan of Massachusetts, then lived, for it was here that he commenced the practice of the law. When once asked by Gen. Knox why he selected such an obscure spot, he replied, that he knew that he must break into the world, and he thought it prudent to make the attempt in a *weak place*."—*Allen.*

drafted from Capt. Hill's company, Col. Scamman's Regiment. He was an ignorant and simple person, and bore in the company to which he belonged the character of a peaceful man. In his letter to Washington, Arnold adds to the foregoing statement, "I wish he may be found a proper object of mercy."

Fort Western stands on the east side of the river Kennebec, and consists of 2 block-houses, and a large house, 100 feet long, which were enclosed only with pickets. This house is the property of [James] Howard, Esq., where we were exceedingly well entertained. Captain Morgan with 3 companies of riflemen embarked in battoes, with orders to proceed with all expedition to the great carrying-place, and clear the road while the other divisions came up.—*Meigs' Journal*, pp. 10, 11. One of the block houses, a venerable memorial of Indian wars, is now [1831] standing, near the covered bridge which stretches across the river. Judge Howard, at whose house the officers were entertained, died in May, 1787, aged 86 years. He was the first commandant at this fort. John Gilley, an irishman, a soldier at the fort under Judge Howard, died at Augusta, Me., July 9th, 1813, aged about 124 years. —*Maine Hist. Soc. Coll.* vol. i, p. 390.

Note D., Page 4.

Sept. 29th. At 11 o'clock, A. M. arrived at Fort Halifax, which stands on a point of land between the river Kennebec and the river Sebasteecook. This fort consists of two large block-houses, and a large barrack, which is enclosed with a picket fort. I tarried half an hour at the fort, then crossed the river to a carrying place, which is 97 rods carriage—then proceeded up the river, which falls very rapidly over a rocky bottom 5 miles, and encamped. The above falls are Toronock.—*Meigs.* Fort Halifax was built by Mr. Shirley in 1754, to awe the Indians, and cover the frontiers of New England.—*Montresor's Journal.*

Note E., Page 5.

October 3d. Proceeded up the river to Norridgewalk. On my way I called at a house, where I saw a child 14 months old. This is the first white child born in Norridgewalk.* At 7 o'clock in the evening, a little below Norridgewalk, my battoe filled with water, going up the falls. Here I lost my kettle, butter and sugar, a loss not to be replaced here. At Norridgewalk are to be seen the vestiges of an

*The name of this child was Abel Farrington. He was the son of Capt. Thomas Farrington, formerly of Groton, Mass.

7

Indian fort and chapel, and a priest's grave.* There appears to have been some intrenchment, and a covered way through the bank of the river for the convenience of getting water. This must have been a considerable seat of the natives, as there are large Indian fields cleared. *Meig's Journal.*

October 4th. Went up to Bumazees Ripples, and came to Norridgewalk. The carriage-place is about a mile in length. We had oxen to haul over our provision. Our batteaux were calked. We were now to take leave of houses and settlements, of which we saw no more, except one Indian wigwam, 'till we came among the French, in Canada. —*Melvin's Journal.*

Note F., Page 16—note.

"In August, 1824, an Indian woman from Penobscot presented herself at my house, with baskets to sell, and soliciting charity. She exhibited a certificate signed by Major General Ulmer, stating that she was the daughter of *Sa Bates*, a Penobscot Indian, who piloted Arnold's army to Quebec in 1775. I asked her to pronounce the name of her father, and she gave the sound—*Sah-Bah-tis.*"—*Allen.*

Note G., Page 24.

Major Timothy Bigelow was the son of Daniel Bigelow, and lived in Worcester, Mass. On hearing of the battle of Lexington, he marched at the head of minute men. In all the fatigues, perils and privations of Arnold's expedition, he participated. At Quebec he was taken prisoner. After his release, he, at the head of the fifteenth Mass. regiment, was at Saratoga, Rhode Island, Valley Forge, and West Point. He was an original grantor of Montpelier, and a liberal benefactor of Leicester Academy. With an ardent temperament, his manners were dignified and graceful. He died in Worcester, March 31, 1790, aged 50 years. Major Bigelow was father of Timothy Bigelow, who removed to Medford in 1807, and was distinguished as a learned, eloquent and popular lawyer, and for more than twenty years as a leading member of the Legislature, eleven of which he served as Speaker of the House of Representatives.

*This was the grave of Father Sebastian Ralle, whom Capt. Thayer, by mistake, calls Francisco. He was a learned man, an effective preacher, and exercised a remarkable influence over the Indians, among whom he dwelt at Norridgewalk, as a Jesuit Missionary, for a period of twenty-six years. He was killed in the surprisal of that place on the 23d August, 1724. A dictionary compiled by him of the Abnâki's language, is preserved among the literary treasures of the library of Harvard College.

Major John Brown was born in Sandisfield, Mass., October 19, 1744. He was educated at Yale College, and after graduating studied law with Oliver Arnold, in Providence, R. I. He established himself in practice at Caghnawaga, now Johnston, N. Y., but at the opening of the revolution took sides with the people against the Mother Country. In 1775 he was a delegate to the Provincial Congress. He was with Arnold at the capture of Ticonderoga, and afterward joined the assaulting forces at Quebec. In 1776 he was commissioned Lieut. Colonel by Congress, and continued in active service until the surrender of Burgoyne. In 1780 he marched up the Mohawk for the relief of Gen. Schuyler, but was led by a traitor into an ambuscade at Stone Arabia, in Palatine, and was slain on his birth-day, October 19, 1780, aged 36 years. He was a man of fine personal presence, and energetic in all his undertakings.

Captain Henry Dearborn was born in Hampton, N. H., March 1, 1751. He studied medicine with Dr. Hall Jackson, of Portsmouth, N. H., and settled in practice at Nottingham square. When an express announced the battle of Lexington, he marched the same day with sixty volunteers for Cambridge. On his return he was commissioned a Captain in Stark's regiment. He raised a company, and participated in the battle of Breed's [or Bunker's] Hill. He joined Arnold in his wilderness march to Quebec, and was seized with fever on the way. He lay in a cottage on the banks of the Chaudiere, without physician, and for ten days his life was despaired of. A good Catholic woman even sprinkled him with holy water. But he gradually recovered, and hastening forward reached Wolfe's Cove in season to rejoin his company, and participate in the assault on Quebec, where he was taken prisoner. In May, 1776, he was paroled, and in March, 1777, was exchanged. He was commissioned Major, in Scammel's regiment, and fought at Ticonderoga and Monmouth; was with Sullivan in his expedition against the Indians in 1779; in 1780 was with the army in New Jersey; in 1781 was at Yorktown, at the surrender of Cornwallis. On the death of Scammel he succeeded to the command of the regiment. In 1782 he was stationed in garrison at Saratoga. After the peace he settled in Maine, of which District he was appointed Marshal. He was twice elected a member of Congress, and was eight years Secretary of War under Jefferson. In the war of 1812 he was commissioned as senior Major General in the army of the United States. In 1815 he retired to private life, and in 1822 was appointed Minister plenipotentiary to Portugal. He died at the residence of his son, General Henry A. S. Dearborn, in Roxbury, Mass., June 6, 1829, aged 78 years.

Colonel CHRISTOPHER GREENE was a lineal descendant of John Greene, who emigrated from Wiltshire, England, to Plymouth Colony, from whence he removed to Providence in 1637. He soon afterwards went to that section of Warwick, R. I., which he had purchased of the aboriginal owners. He was one of the twenty-four individuals to whom Charles the Second granted the old Charter of Rhode Island. His posterity often filled the most responsible stations under the Colonial Government. One of them, William Greene, held the reins of the State during the gloom and horror of the American Revolution; another, upon the Judicial Bench, was the inflexible minister of justice; while two others unsheathed their swords in the service of their country.

Christopher, the subject of this notice, was the son of Hon. Philip Greene, a Judge of the Superior Court of the State, and distinguished alike for his virtues as a private citizen and as a public officer. Christopher was born in 1737, in that part of Warwick called Occupassatiouxet, the patrimonial estate of the Judge, his father. His life, previously to entering the army, was principally occupied in agriculture, and in the care of a grist and saw mill, located on a branch of the Pawtuxet river, at what is now called Centreville. His natural endowments were of a superior order. His mental powers, improved and developed by education and refined social intercourse, together with an elevated moral character, were calculated to command the confidence of his fellow-citizens, and at an early age he was elected by them to represent his town in the State Legislature, an office which he honorably filled for several years. At this time, the Mother country began to seize, one after another, the inherent rights of the Colonies. When the question of resistance came to be discussed, young Greene boldly took ground against the King, and his counsels in the Legislature tended to encourage measures for military defence.

A military company was established at East Greenwich, in 1774, with the title of "Kentish Guards," and Greene was chosen Lieutenant. In the month of May, 1775, he was appointed by the Legislature a Major in the army created for the defence of the State, under the command of his near relative and intimate friend, General Nathaniel Greene. But, with characteristic self-denying patriotism, he preferred to accept the office of Captain in the regiment organized by the General Assembly for the Continental service, which opened to him a field for more active usefulness. He marched to Cambridge, and was there placed as Lieutenant Colonel in command of the first battalion of Arnold's army, formed for a secret expedition against Quebec. The duties of this new and responsible position were discharged with the utmost faithfulness. Through the entire wilderness march, his constant presence and cheerful voice inspired the courage and hope of his men. In the attack upon Quebec, Lieutenant Colonel Greene took a conspicuous part. At the head of an assaulting column of infantry, he was in the midst of the hottest conflict. But the early death of General Montgomery changed the fortunes of a day auspiciously begun, and after three hours of hard fighting, Greene and his command were compelled to surrender.

Eighteen months of prison life passed heavily with the active spirit of Colonel Greene. His thoughts were with his suffering country, and his uppermost desire was to again draw his sword in her behalf. On one occasion, when contemplating the British flag waving tauntingly above him, and listening to the triumph-strains of British music, his self-possession forsook him, and he exclaimed, with emphatic tone, "*I will never again be taken prisoner alive!*"—a declaration never forgotten by those who heard it, and that became a proverb with the soldiers who had served under him.

The value of the services of Lieutenant Colonel Greene and of his fellow-officers, were fully appreciated by General Washington, and in a letter to Governor Cooke, dated "Head-quarters, Harlem Heights, Oct. 12, 1776, he stated that their behaviour and merits, as well as the severities they had experienced in the Canada Expedition, entitled them to particular notice, and recommended that, in the new levies then about to be raised by the State, vacancies should be reserved for them, to be filled upon their exchange. Colonel Varnum, writing to the Governor from West Chester, October 16, on the same subject, says: "How the Field Officers are recommended for the First Battallion in our State, and who they are, I am ignorant. I hope Colonel Greene will be thought of."

After being exchanged, Lieut. Colonel Greene, in 1777, received a commission of Colonel, and was placed in command of the highly important post of Fort Mercer, at Red Bank, on the Delaware river. This position was attacked by a large body of Germans under Colonel Count Donop, who, after a fierce and desperate fight, were driven back defeated, with heavy loss, including their commander.* Colonel

* "The late Dr. Turner, of Newport, who was in this battle, used to narrate the following anecdote of Col. Greene's kind attention to a vanquished enemy. He buried the remains of Count Donop with all the honors of war. A Frenchman, the

Jonathan Mifflin, in a letter to General Mifflin, dated "Headquarters, G. Morris's, Oct. 24, 1777, 5 o'clock, P. M.," says: "The day before yesterday, 4 o'clock P. M., Count Donop, with 1200 Hessian Grenadiers, made their appearance before the garrison at Red Bank, and by flag demanded a surrender, which being refused, they made an immediate attack, fired above the abattis, crossed the ditch, and some few had mounted the pickets. They were so warmly received that they returned with great precipitation, leaving behind the Count and the Brigade Major, who are wounded, in the fort." The killed and wounded, according to this letter, were 500. The same writer continues: "Colonel Greene, who commanded, played upon them a very good deception. When the flag came in, he concealed all his men but 50—saying, "*with these brave fellows, this fort shall be my tomb.*"—He had 5 killed and 45 wounded."

Commodore John Hazlewood writing to Gen. Washington, under date Red Bank, Oct. 24, 1777, says, "This will acquaint your Excellency that early this morning we carried all our gallies into action, and, after a long and heavy firing, we drove the enemy's ships down the river, except a 64 gun ship and a small frigate, which we obliged them to quit, as they got on shore, and by accident the 64 gun ship blew up, and the frigate they set on fire themselves, took the people all out, and quitted them. Our action lasted until 12 o'clock, and our fleet has received but little damage.

"You will be informed of the glorious event of last night, by Col. Greene. We, in our gallies, were of great use in flanking round the fort. Besides the 64 and frigate being burnt, the Roebuck, which lay to cover them, we damaged much and drove off, and had she laid fast, we should have had her in the same situation."

"The success of Col. Greene the day before, it is fair to infer, contributed much to the naval successes of the day following, and finally to the enemy abandoning Philadelphia, thus breaking down, in an eminent degree, their warlike power.

---

surgeon of the German Brigade, who was taken prisoner, on witnessing the American troops following the corpse of his beloved commander, and depositing it, with every manifestation of respect, in the grave, was so affected by the unexpected spectacle that, springing up and striking his feet together, he exclaimed, with the vivacity of his countrymen, "De Gar, if dey bury me so, I die dis moment."—Rather an odd, but certainly a very striking illustration of his devotedness to Donop, and his gratitude to Greene."—*Note to a sketch of Col. Greene in the Kent County Atlas, Nov. 8 and 15, 1851, by Hon. H. Rousmaniere, of which use has been made in this notice.*

In January, after the battle of Red Bank, a letter was written to Gen. Washington, by Gen. J. M. Varnum, dated "Camp, January 2, 1778," in which he says: "The two Battalions for the State being small, and there being a necessity of the State's furnishing an additional number to make up their proportion in the Continental Army, the Field Officers have represented to me the propriety of making one temporary Battalion from the two, so that one entire corps of officers may repair to Rhode Island, in order to receive and prepare the recruits for the field. It is imagined that a Battalion of negroes may be raised there. . . . . . The Field Officers who go upon this command, are Col. Greene, Lt. Col. Olney, and Major Ward."

Colonel Greene, after this, was employed in Rhode Island for a period of the war, from 1778 to 1780, and had a spirited fight with the enemy on the Island, in which the negro troops distinguished themselves. He coöperated with the French fleet and army, the former under Count D'Estaing, the latter under the command of General Count Rochambeau. In 1781, he returned to the headquarters of Gen. Washington, and on the night of the 13th of May, was attacked at his quarters near Croton Bridge, Croton River, N. Y., by a party of refugees, overpowered, and barbarously murdered. His left arm was cut off, his right wounded to the bone in two wide gashes, his left shoulder severely mutilated, his stomach pierced by a sword, his right side shockingly lacerated by a bayonet, and his head mangled in several places. In this condition, he was dragged by the ruffians who had overpowered him, to a wood about a mile distant, and there left.

General Washington learned, with the deepest sorrow, the details of the melancholy fate of his honored friend and brother in arms. His corpse was carried to the headquarters of the army on the subsequent day, and buried with every token of military honor, and every semblance of individual grief.* General Rochambeau took occasion to remark in a letter to Gov. Greene, dated at Newport, 27th May, 1781, "Your Excellency will, I hope, be persuaded how much I lament the loss of your friend and relative, Col. Greene. I had the greatest esteem and regard for an officer of such merit." At the October Session of the General Assembly, 1785, seven years' half pay was allowed to the widow and children of Col. Greene, dating from the day of his death.

---

*Both Colonel Greene and Major Flagg, who was murdered at the same time, were buried in the church-yard at Compond, where a tomb stone was erected. Compond was about seven miles from Peekskill.

The gallant defence of Fort Mercer, at Red Bank, gave to Colonel Greene a prominent military reputation, and Congress was prompt to recognize the brilliant deed by passing a resolution, Nov. 4, 1777, "That an elegant sword be provided by the Board of War, and presented to Col. Greene." The execution of this complimentary resolve was delayed until several years after the death of the Colonel, when the sword was forwarded to Job Greene, Esq., the son and legal representative of the deceased, accompanied with the following letter:

"WAR OFFICE OF THE UNITED STATES,
New York, June 7, 1786.

SIR:

I have the honor to transmit to you, the son and legal representative of the late memorable and gallant Col. Greene, the sword directed to be presented to him, by the resolve of Congress of the 4th of November, 1777.

"The repulse and defeat of the Germans at the Fort of Red Bank, on the Delaware, is justly considered as one of the most brilliant actions of the late war. The glory of that event is inseparably attached to the memory of your father and his brave garrison. The manner in which the supreme authority of the United States is pleased to express its high sense of his military merit, and the honorable instrument which they annex in testimony thereof, must be peculiarly precious to a son emulative of his father's virtues. The circumstances of the war prevented obtaining and delivery of the sword previous to your father's being killed at Croton River, in 1780. [1.]

"On that catastrophe, his country mourned the sacrifice of a patriot and a soldier, and mingled its tears with those of his family. That the patriotic and military virtues of your honorable father may influence your conduct in every case in which your country may require your services, is the sincere wish,

Sir,
Of your most obedient
and very humble servant,
H. KNOX.

Job Greene, Esq."

This sword is now in the possession of one of the grandchildren of Colonel Greene, Simon Henry Greene, Esq., of River Point, R. I. Its sheath is of rattle-snake skin, the blade a polished rapier, and its principle decorations of silver, inlaid with gold. At the time of his death, Col. Greene had entered upon his forty-fifth year. In 1758, he married Miss Anne Lippitt, the daughter of Mr. Jeremiah Lippitt, of

Warwick. He left three sons and four daughters. His portrait, belonging to Simon Henry Greene, Esq., exhibits the appearance of a man who would do effectual service on the battle-field. Under the laborious exercise of the farm and the camp, he ripened into a rare combination of symmetrical figure and solid expression. His height was about five feet ten inches. His round, capacious chest, his upright mien, his active, muscular limbs, indicated the enjoyment of perfect physical vigor. Dark brown hair clustered around his forehead, which bespoke deep thought rather than brilliant fancy. There was a strange lustre in his eyes that would have given the expression of life to a face of clay. The outline of his features was grave and stern, as if it were but a transparent veil over his restless mind; while his entire countenance was lit up with a ruddy, sanguine complexion, through which coursing blood looked out to tell the story of inward health and joyousness. A copy of this portrait was a few years since painted at the expense of the State of Rhode Island, and was made one of a growing gallery of her eminent sons and benefactors now formed in the Hall of Brown University. Col. Greene died at an age when his military

Corrections. Page 57, line 16 from top. The portrait of Colonel Greene was presented to the gallery in the Hall of Brown University, by Simon Henry Greene, Esq., and was not painted at the expense of the State, as inadvertently stated.

Page 87, line 2 from bottom, for Louis XIV, read "Louis XVI."

Soon after this gallant corps marched to Cambridge, Lieutenant Hubbard was appointed Captain, and, when the expedition against Quebec was planned, he was assigned to a company in the detachment of Arnold. While the troops halted at Fort Western on the Kennebec, he wrote to his wife in terms worthy of a patriot martyr: "I know not if I shall ever see you again. The weather grows severe cold, and the woods, they say, are terrible to pass. But I do not value life or property, if I can secure liberty for my children." Captain Hubbard shared in the extreme sufferings of the march, and probably

The gallant defence of Fort Mercer, at Red Bank, gave to Colonel Greene a prominent military reputation, and Congress was prompt to recognize the brilliant deed by passing a resolution, Nov. 4, 1777, "That an elegant sword be provided by the Board of War, and presented to Col. Greene." The execution of this complimentary resolve was delayed until several years after the death of the Colonel, when the sword was forwarded to Job Greene, Esq., the son and legal representative of the deceased, accompanied with the following letter:

"WAR OFFICE OF THE UNITED STATES,
New York, June 7, 1786.

SIR:

I have the honor to transmit to you, the son and legal representative of the late memorable and gallant Col. Greene, the sword directed to be presented to him, by the resolve of Congress of the 4th of November, 1777.

"The repulse and defeat of the Germans at the Fort of Red Bank, on the Delaware, is justly considered as one of the most brilliant

Of your most obedient
and very humble servant,
H. KNOX.

Job Greene, Esq."

This sword is now in the possession of one of the grandchildren of Colonel Greene, Simon Henry Greene, Esq., of River Point, R. I. Its sheath is of rattle-snake skin, the blade a polished rapier, and its principle decorations of silver, inlaid with gold. At the time of his death, Col. Greene had entered upon his forty-fifth year. In 1758, he married Miss Anne Lippitt, the daughter of Mr. Jeremiah Lippitt, of

Warwick. He left three sons and four daughters. His portrait, belonging to Simon Henry Greene, Esq., exhibits the appearance of a man who would do effectual service on the battle-field. Under the laborious exercise of the farm and the camp, he ripened into a rare combination of symmetrical figure and solid expression. His height was about five feet ten inches. His round, capacious chest, his upright mien, his active, muscular limbs, indicated the enjoyment of perfect physical vigor. Dark brown hair clustered around his forehead, which bespoke deep thought rather than brilliant fancy. There was a strange lustre in his eyes that would have given the expression of life to a face of clay. The outline of his features was grave and stern, as if it were but a transparent veil over his restless mind; while his entire countenance was lit up with a ruddy, sanguine complexion, through which coursing blood looked out to tell the story of inward health and joyousness. A copy of this portrait was a few years since painted at the expense of the State of Rhode Island, and was made one of a growing gallery of her eminent sons and benefactors now formed in the Hall of Brown University. Col. Greene died at an age when his military experience, maturity of judgment, and energy of character, gave promise of rapid promotion. Had he lived to the close of the war, his rank, probably, would have been second only to that of his distinguished kinsman.

Captain Jonas Hubbard, the son of an early settler in Worcester, Mass., was born in that town. Previous to the Revolution, he was engaged in the cultivation of his patrimonial estate, and in the management of extensive concerns of business. The first sounds of coming war found him an Ensign in one of the three militia companies of the town. When the volunteer company of minute men was raised, Hubbard was elected Lieutenant, and actively participated in the evening drills after the labors of the day were over, and in the preparations made by the busy industry of the martial spirit of the times, for immediate action.

Soon after this gallant corps marched to Cambridge, Lieutenant Hubbard was appointed Captain, and, when the expedition against Quebec was planned, he was assigned to a company in the detachment of Arnold. While the troops halted at Fort Western on the Kennebec, he wrote to his wife in terms worthy of a patriot martyr: "I know not if I shall ever see you again. The weather grows severe cold, and the woods, they say, are terrible to pass. But I do not value life or property, if I can secure liberty for my children." Captain Hubbard shared in the extreme sufferings of the march, and probably more than his proportion, as, acting under a commission among those who had no reverence for artificial distinctions, beyond that yielded to the legitimate authority of courage and wisdom.

In the attack on Quebec, Captain Hubbard fell, at the head of his company, severely wounded. Respected for his fearless intrepidity, and loved for his personal worth, his men wished to remove him to a place of shelter from the fast falling snow, and of safety from the vollies of balls poured down from the ramparts. But he peremptorily refused. 'I came here to serve with you, I will stay here to die with you,' were his last words to a comrade who survived. Bleeding and stretched on a bed of ice, exposed to the bitter influence of a winter storm, life soon departed. It was a glorious time and place for the gallant soldier to yield up his breath, beneath the massive walls of the impregnable citadel, with the death shot flying fast, and the thunder of battle swelling round him. The sons of Captain Hubbard, inheriting his adventurous and manly spirit, emigrated to Maine, where the eldest, Gen. Levi Hubbard, became the first settler of Paris. Gen. Hubbard held many offices with honor, and was representative of Oxford District in Congress, from 1813 to 1815.—*Lincoln's History of Worcester.*

JOHN JOSEPH HENRY was the son of William and Ann Wood Henry, of Lancaster, Penn. William, (whose parents emigrated from Coleraine, Ireland,) was a distinguished Whig during the Revolution, and had an extensive manufactory of arms, established previously to the French War. In 1777, he was Deputy Commissary General, and was active in sending supplies to the army at Valley Forge. In 1784, he was elected to Congress, and died Dec. 15, 1786.

JOHN JOSEPH was born in Lancaster, Penn., Nov. 4th, 1758, and early manifested marked mechanical genius. At the age of 14, he became an apprentice to his uncle at the gunsmith business, who subsequently removed to Detroit. Here young Henry remained but a short time, and returned home on foot through the wilderness. His ardent mind panted for military glory, and sympathising warmly with his struggling country, he, at the age of 16 years, clandestinely enlisted in a company raised by Captain Matthew Smith, for the purpose of joining Arnold's Expedition against Quebec. His sufferings on the march through the wilderness were extreme. He was captured in the attack upon Quebec, and lay in prison nine months, where he contracted the scurvy, which made its appearance on his return home, in a malignant form, from the effects of which he never entirely recovered. Mr. Henry spoke the German language, and while in prison was approached by Captain Prentis, in behalf of Gen. Knyphausen, then at Quebec, with the offer of a place in his military family, as an interpreter. The offer was declined.

He sailed from Quebec Aug. 10, 1776, and after a voyage of four weeks, reached New York. Of his advent into Elizabethtown, a few days after, he gives the following description: "It was ten or eleven at night before we landed. The moon shone beautifully. Morgan stood in the bow of the boat, making a spring not easily surpassed, and falling on the earth, as it were to grasp it,—cried, "Oh, my country." We that were near him, pursued his example. Now a race commenced, which in quickness, could scarcely be exceeded, and soon brought us to Elizabethtown. Here, those of us who were drowsy spent an uneasy night. Being unexpected guests, and the town full of troops, no quarters were provided for us. Joy rendered beds useless. We did not close our eyes till daylight. Singing, dancing, the Indian halloo, in short, every species of vociferousness was adopted by the men and many of the most respectable sergeants, to express their extreme pleasure. A stranger coming among them, would have pronounced them mad, or at least intoxicated, though since noon neither food nor liquor had passed our lips. Thus the passions may, at times, have an influence on the human frame, as inebriating as wine or any other liquor. The morning brought us plenty, in the form of rations of beef and bread. Hunger allayed, my desire was to proceed homewards."

On reaching home, a Lieutenancy in the Pennsylvania Line was offered Mr. Henry, and also a Captaincy in the Virginia Line. The latter he designed to accept, under Morgan, but the state of his health prevented. Continued lameness precluded all possibility of his again entering the army, and he indentured himself for four years as a clerk in the prothonotary's office of Lancaster County, and made himself master of its duties. He subsequently studied law, under Stephen Chambers, Esq., whose youngest sister he afterwards married. Mr. Henry engaged successfully in the practice of law, from 1785 to the close of 1793, when his well known legal abilities were rewarded with an appointment by Governor Thomas Mifflin, to the office of President of the Second Judicial District of Pennsylvania. This position he held seventeen years, when, from illness and increasing infirmities, he felt it a duty to resign. Four months after, he died. Judge Henry wrote an interesting and valuable narrative of the Campaign against Quebec, which was published in 1812, and which has frequently been referred to in the preceding pages.

Captain WILLIAM HENDRICKS, from Pennsylvania, was tall, of a mild and beautiful countenance. His soul was animated by a genuine spark of heroism. He was active and energetic in the march through the wilderness, and shared freely in the toils and privations of his men. When it became necessary to transport Lieutenant McCleland, of his company, in a litter across the mountains, he took his turn with the men. "If you had seen," says Henry, "the young yet venerable Captain Hendricks, bearing his share of this loved burthen across the plain to our camp, it would have raised esteem, if not affection, towards him." He was no stickler for rank where the harmony of the service was involved. Morgan had obtained the command of the rifle corps from Arnold, without any advertence to the better claim of Hendricks, who, though the youngest man, was, of the three Captains, in point of rank, by the dates of commissions, the superior officer. For the sake of peace in the army, and of good order, he prudently and good naturedly acquiesced in Morgan's assumption of the command. He was conspicuous in the assault upon Quebec, and, as mentioned in the Introduction, was killed by a straggling ball received through the heart.

Captain JOHN LAMB, son of Anthony Lamb, a celebrated optician and mathematical instrument maker, in New York, was born in that city, January 1, 1735. In early life, he followed the profession of his father. About 1760, he commenced the business of a wine merchant, and nearly at the same time, married Catherine Jandine, a lady of Huguenot descent. He improved his opportunities for mental culture, spoke the French and German languages, was a pleasant speaker and forcible writer. In the beginning of the troubles that led on to Revolution, Mr. Lamb sided with the country, and became a prominent member of the New York Sons of Liberty. Early in 1775, he offered his services to Congress, and was commissioned a Captain of Artillery, a position for which his military studies fitted him. For a time, he was stationed, with his company, on the Battery, in New York; but when the invasion of Canada, by Generals Schuyler and Montgomery, was determined upon, he marched and joined the invading army, at the Isle-aux-Noix. When St. John's capitulated, Capt. Lamb and his company, with two hundred other men, were ordered to march into town to receive the surrender of the fort and take possession. In the subsequent movements, he showed himself an intelligent, energetic and reliable officer. He first met Colonel Arnold before Quebec, and was associated with him in the assault upon that city. He fought with great bravery, was severely wounded, and taken prisoner.

A grape shot hit Lamb on the left cheek, near the eye, the sight of which was ultimately lost, and carried away a part of the bone. The

Your Affectionate Friend
John Lamb.

force of the blow and the concussion of the shot, stunned him, and threw him senseless on the snow. Some of his faithful followers carried him into a cooper's shop near at hand, and laid him upon a pile of shavings insensible.

In searching for the dead and wounded, Capt. Lamb was found where he had been left, still without consciousness, benumbed with cold and loss of blood. A surgeon, after examination, pronounced him yet alive, and made preparations to restore him to animation. A Scottish commissary present, who knew Capt. Lamb, and was familiar with some of his exploits that had made him obnoxious to British ire, suggested that it would be better to let him die, as, if he was recovered, the King's vengeance would certainly be visited upon him. But the suggestion was not accepted. Capt. Lamb was revived and carried to the convent of the nuns of the order of Mercy, then a temporary hospital; not, however, without being plundered of his shoes and buckles, by some of the underlings; and, without shoes, supported by two men, he was assisted over the paved court, covered with snow, and put to bed in that condition, in his wet garments. He recovered slowly, but through life suffered inconvenience from rigidity of the jaw.

Before being released, Capt. Lamb was appointed by Washington to be second Major in the regiment of Artillery commanded by Colonel Henry Knox. He was subsequently made Lieutenant Colonel. He was in command of the Artillery at West Point, when Arnold's treachery and flight was discovered, and was filled with indignation when the disclosure was made. He had been in the most friendly relations with Arnold, but this event caused an instantaneous revulsion of feeling. By one of the numerous flags which passed the lines on the occasion of the capture of André, the officer who brought it was charged to present the regards of Gen. Arnold to Col. Lamb. "Be good enough, sir," was the reply, "to tell Gen. Arnold that the acquaintance between us is forgotten, and that, if he were to be hanged to-morrow, I would go barefooted to witness his execution."

In the battle at Compo Hill, Conn., in 1777, Col. Lamb was struck by a grape shot and severely wounded. After the wound had been dressed, he was taken to the house of Mr. Simpson, temporarily resident of Norwalk, and afterwards to Col. Deming's, at Fairfield. As soon as it was prudent to move, he repaired to New Haven and took command of that place, which had been, in the absence of Gen. Arnold, confided to Lieut. Colonel Oswald. Col. Lamb fought gallantly at Yorktown, but did not secure the reward of promotion that his friends with good reason expected he would. After leaving the army, in which he had made an honorable record, he was elected a member of the New York General Assembly, and took a prominent and influential part in public affairs. He was also raised to the rank of Brigadier General. He was appointed Collector of the Customs for the Port of New York, the duties of which office he discharged with scrupulous fidelity, but the embezzlement of a clerk in whom he imposed entire confidence, involved him in pecuniary ruin. The reimbursement of the loss absorbed his entire fortune, and he retired from office in poverty and distress but with the warm sympathy of both friends and political opponents. General Lamb was an original member of the Society of Cincinnati, and had been twice Vice-President of that body. He died in New York, May 31st, 1800, aged 65 years, and was buried in Trinity Church Yard, with the military honors which he had so well deserved; and the long array of citizens, as they attended him to the tomb, attested the respect which his virtues, his bravery, and worth had universally commanded.* A very interesting Life of Gen. Lamb, by Isaac Q. Leake, was published by Joel Munsell, Albany, in 1850. The press of Mr. Munsell has become celebrated for elegant editions of rare works.

General RICHARD MONTGOMERY was a native of the North of Ireland, and was born in the year 1737. Choosing the profession of arms, he entered the British service, and, as Captain of a company in the 17th Regiment of foot, he fought under General Wolfe in the assault upon Quebec, in 1759. He returned to England, and in 1772, retired from the army. Coming again to America, he settled in New York and married a daughter of Judge Livingston. He was an officer of superior military ability, and but for his untimely death, would doubtless have rendered the country invaluable services. Few officers were so universally beloved by his men, or held in warmer regard by all who knew him.

"All enmity to Montgomery expired with his life, and the respect to his private character prevailed over all other considerations. . . . . The most powerful speakers in the British Parliament displayed their eloquence in praising his virtues, and lamenting his fate. A great orator, and veteran fellow-soldier of his in the late war, shed abundance of tears whilst he expatiated on their past friendship and participation

---

*Several writers state that Capt. Lamb and his company, formed a part of Arnold's force, in the expedition by the Kennebec and Chandiere rivers. This error originated, perhaps, in the fact that Lamb fought under Arnold's command in the attack on Quebec, and his connection with Montgomery being generally unknown.

of service in that season of enterprise and glory. Even the minister extolled his virtues."—*Annual Register for* 1776.*

Major Return J. Meigs was born in Middletown, Ct., in 1740. Soon after the battle of Lexington, he marched a company of infantry to the neighborhood of Boston, and received the commission of Major. He was assigned to Arnold's command, and showed great energy as an officer in the march through the wilderness against Quebec. He fought bravely in the assault upon that place and was taken prisoner. Upon being exchanged, he returned home, and in 1777 was appointed Colonel. For a brilliant expedition to Long Island that year, he received the thanks of Congress and a sword. In 1779, he commanded a regiment under Wayne at the capture of Stony Point. After the war he removed to Ohio, and settled near the confluence of the Ohio and Muskingum rivers. As early as 1816 he was the agent for Indian affairs. He died at the Cherokee agency. His christian name, *Return*, was given him by his father, in commemoration of the happy termination of an interview with a fair Quakeress who at first rejected his suit; but, on taking his departure, she sweetly called to him, saying, "*return, Jonathan*," and consented to become his bride.

Capt. Daniel Morgan was born in New Jersey in 1737, and in 1755 emigrated to Virginia, where he was employed first as a farmer, and afterwards as a wagoner. He shared in the perils of Braddock's expedition against the Indians, and received a wound in his neck and cheek. At the commencement of the Revolutionary war he cast his lot with the sons of freedom, and raised a company of riflemen. In the assault upon Quebec he was in the hottest of the fight. On being exchanged he rejoined the army, and received the command of a regiment. He fought with Gates at Saratoga, and with Greene in the South. He was made brevet Brigadier General. For his bravery at the battle of the Cowpens, Jan. 1, 1781, Congress voted him a gold medal. In the Whiskey Insurrection, Washington called him to command the militia of Virginia. He was afterwards elected a member of Congress. He died at Winchester, Va., after a long and painful sickness, in 1799.

Captain Eleazer Oswald was from New Haven, Conn. He served under Arnold at Ticonderoga, and volunteering to accompany him through the wilderness to Quebec, was made secretary to his commander. In the assault upon that place, he led a forlorn hope, and exhibited great courage. He was taken prisoner, and after being

*See Introduction.

exchanged, received the appointment of Lieutenant Colonel in Colonel Lamb's regiment of Artillery. For a short time he was stationed at New Haven, with such recruits as he had been enabled to collect. From thence he proceeded to Providence, to secure the services of an accomplished musician who he had learned might be obtained there, and also to promote enlistments. On arriving at Providence he found that the fifer had been recently promoted to a Majority in the line of the army, and consequently, as he wrote, "above that business." In a short time he returned to Connecticut, and, during the temporary absence of Col. Lamb, took charge of the affairs of the regiment. He was in the affair at Compo, and afterwards with part of two companies and three field pieces, joined Arnold at Norwalk. He was subsequently with his regiment at Peekskill, where, receiving personal indignity from Gen. Putnam, he determined to resign, but through the influence of friends, was induced to forego his purpose. Lieut. Col. Oswald participated in the battle of Monmouth, and for his gallant services received the commendations of Generals Knox and Lee. In August, 1778, being unjustly outranked, through the enmity of Gen. Gates, who disliked him on account ot his devotion to Washington, he resigned his commission. After leaving the army, he entered into the printing and publishing business in Philadelphia, was appointed public printer, and was a resident of that city during the time it was under the command of Arnold. The treason of that officer drew from Oswald several indignant letters. In a letter to Col. Lamb, he said: "Happy for him, and for his friends, it had been, had the ball which pierced his leg at Saratoga, been directed through his heart; he then would have finished his career in glory, but the remainder of his wretched existence, must now be one continued scene of horror, misery and despair. . . . . He has convinced the world that he is as base a prostitute as this or any other country ever nurtured to maturity, and as a punishment for the enormity of his crimes, the mark of Cain is branded on him in the most indelible characters."

In the political discussions of the times, Lieut. Col. Oswald took an active part, and, under extraordinary provocation, sent a challenge to Col. Hamilton, which, upon satisfactory explanation, was withdrawn. During the French Revolution he went to England on business, and, guided by his natural enthusiasm for liberty and passion for military renown, crossed the channel and entered the army of Dumourier. He was placed in command of a regiment of artillery, and served with credit in the battle of Mons or Jemappe. He returned to his native land, and in October, 1795, died of small pox, contracted while nursing a friend who had been fatally attacked by that pestilence. On the 2d of October he was buried in St. Paul's church yard, in New York.

Rev. SAMUEL SPRING, the chaplain of Arnold's detachment, was born in Northbridge, Mass., February 27, 1746, and was educated at Princeton College, where he graduated in 1771. On his return from Quebec he left the army, and August 6, 1777, received ordination. He was a minister for many years in Newburyport, Mass., and was an attractive preacher. He was one of the founders of the Massachusetts Missionary Society in 1799, and also of the Andover Theological Seminary, and the American Board of Commissioners for Foreign Missions. His publications were numerous. He died March 4, 1819, aged 73 years. His son, Rev. Gardner Spring, D.D., has long been one of the prominent clergymen of New York.

Captain MATTHEW SMITH commanded a company from Lancaster county, Penn. Henry, who served under him, says, "he was a good looking man, had the air of a soldier, but was illiterate, and outrageously talkative." Previous to the assault upon Quebec, he was present by invitation of General Montgomery, at a council of officers. On one occasion, in the march through the wilderness, he saved a soldier who had violated an order prohibiting the firing of guns, from summary punishment by Morgan. The soldier denied having committed the offence. Morgan, in a momentary passion, seized a billet of wood and threatened to knock him down unless he confessed the fact. Whereupon Smith seized another billet and threatened to serve Morgan in like manner if he struck the man. Morgan knowing the tenure of his rank, receded.

Dr. ISAAC SENTER was born in Londonderry, in the State of New Hampshire, in the year 1753. Of his boyhood life no particulars are preserved. Choosing the Healing Art for a profession, he went to Newport, R. I., and engaged in the study of medicine, under the direction of Dr. Thomas Moffat, a Scotch physician of eminence. The ardor with which he pursued his studies did not render him indifferent to the important events then transpiring. Every fibre of his heart was patriotic, and when the tidings of the battle of Lexington reached Newport, he instantly joined the Rhode Island troops as a volunteer surgeon, and accompanied them to the camp of the American army in Cambridge. He soon after received an appointment of surgeon in the Continental line, and was assigned to the detachment under Arnold for the Canada expedition. Dr. Senter was now twenty-two years of age, and his new position opened to him a wide field for gathering medical and surgical experience. His life, on the memorable march through the wilderness to Quebec, was replete with adventure, while frequent demands were made on his professional services. Cheerful and hopeful under multiplied discouragements, he pressed on with his companions, at one time wading through swamps, sinking half-leg deep in the mire at every step, and at another feeding on "the jawbone of a swine destitute of any covering, boiled in a quantity of water with a little thickening;" but all the way invulnerable to persuasions to turn back. As a specimen of his experience, the following extracts from his Journal are given:

Tuesday, Oct. 24th.—Approaching necessity now obliged us to double our diligence. Three miles only had we proceeded ere we came to a troublesome waterfall in the river, distant half a mile. Not more than the last mentioned distance before we were brought up by another, distance the same. As the number of falls increased, the water became consequently more rapid. The heights of land upon each side of the river, which had hitherto been inconsiderable, now became prodigiously mountainous, closing as it were up the river with an aspect of an immense height. The river was now become very narrow, and such a horrid current as rendered it impossible to proceed in any other method than by hauling the batteaux up by the bushes, painters, &c. Here we met several boats returning loaded with invalids, and lamentable stories of the inaccessibleness of the river, and the impracticability of any further progress into the country. Among which was Mr. Jackson, before mentioned, complaining of the gout most severely, joined to all the terrors of approaching famine. I was now exhorted in the most pathetic terms to return, on pain of famishing upon contrary conduct, and the army were all returning except a few who were many miles forward with Col. Arnold. However, his elocution did not prevail; I therefore bid him adieu and proceeded. Not far had I proceeded before I discovered several wrecks of batteaux belonging to the front division of riflemen, &c., with an increased velocity of the water. A direful, howling wilderness not describable. With much labour and difficulty, I arrived with the principal part of my baggage (leaving the batteaux made fast) to the encampment. Two miles from thence I met the informants last mentioned, where were Col. Greene's division, &c., waiting for the remainder of the army to come up, that they might get some provisions, ere they advanced any further. Upon inquiry, I found them almost destitute of any eatable whatever, except a few *candles*, which were used for supper, and breakfast the next morning, by boiling them in water gruel, &c.

Wednesday, 25th.—Every prospect of distress now came thundering on with a two-fold rapidity. A storm of snow had covered the ground of nigh six inches deep, attended with very severe weather. We now waited in anxious expectation for Col. Enos' division to come up, in order that we might have a recruit of provisions ere we could start off the ground. An express was ordered both up and down the river, the one up the river in quest of Col. Arnold, that he might be informed of the state of the army, many of whom were now entirely destitute of any sustenance. The Col. had left previous orders for the two divisions, viz: Greene's and Enos', to come to an adjustment of the provisions—send back any who were indisposed, either in body or mind, and pursue him with the others immediately. The other express went down the river to desire Col. Enos and officers to attend in consultation. They accordingly came up before noon, when a council of war was ordered. Here sat a number of grimacers—melancholy aspects who had been preaching to their men the doctrine of impenetrability and non-perseverance. Col. Enos in the chair. The matter was debated upon the expediency of proceeding on for Quebec. The party against going urging the impossibility, averring the whole provisions, when averaged, would not support the army five days.

The arrangements of men and provisions were made at Fort Western, in such a manner as to proceed with the greater expedition. For this end, it was thought necessary that Capt. Morgan's company, with a few pioneers, should advance in the first division, Col. Greene's in the second, and Enos, with Capt. Colbourn's company of artificers, to bring up the rear. The advantage of the arrangement was very conspicuous, as the rear division would not only have the roads cut, rivers cleared passable for boats, &c., but stages or encampments formed and the bough huts remaining for the rear. The men being thus arranged, the provisions were distributed according to the supposed difficulty, or facility, attending the different dispositions. Many of the first companies took only two or three barrels of flour with several of bread, most in a small proportion. While the companies in the last division had not less than fourteen of flour and ten of bread. The bread, as mentioned before, was condemned in consequence of the leaky casks, therefore the proportion of bread being much greater in the first division, their loss was consequently the greater. These hints being premised, I now proceed to the determination of the council of war. After debating upon the state of the army with respect to provisions, there was found very little in the division then encamped at the falls, (which I shall name *Hydrophobus*.) The other companies not being come up, either through fear that they should be obliged to come to a divider, or to show their disapprobation of proceeding any further. The question being put whether all to return, or only part, the majority were for part only returning. Part only of the officers of those detachments were in this council.

According to Col. Arnold's recommendation, the invalids were allowed to return, as also the timorous. The officers who were for going forward, requested a division of the provisions, and that it was necessary they should have the far greater quantity in proportion to the number of men, as the supposed distance that they had to go ere they arrived into the inhabitants was greater than what they had come, after leaving the Cenebec inhabitants. To this the returning party (being pre-determined) would not consent, alledging that they would either go back with what provisions they had, or if they must go forward they'd not impart any. Col. Enos, though [he] voted for proceeding, yet had undoubtedly prefngaged to the contrary, as every action demonstrated. To compel them to a just division, we were not in a situation, as being the weakest party. Expostulations and entreaties had hitherto been fruitless. Col. Enos, who more immediately commanded the division of *returners*, was called upon to give positive orders for a small quantity, if no more. He replied that his men were out of his power, and that they had determined to keep their possessed quantity whether they went back or forward. They finally concluded to spare [us] 2½ barrels of flour, if determined to pursue our destination; adding that we never should be able to bring [in] any inhabitants. Thus circumstanced, we were left the alternative of accepting their small pittance, and proceed, or return. The former was adopted, with a determined resolution to go through or die. Received it, put it on board of our boats, quit the few tents we were in possession of, with all other camp equipage, took each man to his duds on his back, bid them adieu, and away—passed the river; passed over falls and encamped.

Monday, 30th.—Cooking being very much out of fashion, we had little else to do than march as quick as light permitted; half an hour only brought us to a water which we imagined to be a creek formed by the lake; laid our course more southwardly, endeavoring to go round it, but three miles march evinced our mistake; our creek proved to be a river of four rods wide. The depth and width of this river rendered it unfordable, nor [was] it possible to form a bridge, as nothing of any bigness grew on its banks. It was now conjectured this river made out of the Alleghany chain of mountains, which we had therefore the marching round it impracticable. We therefore concluded to proceed up it till it was fordable. We had not gone far before we came to a place about four feet deep, which we immediately forded, although much frozen on each side. This *Balneum Frigidum* served to exercise our motion in order to keep from freezing. Our main course was W. N. W., and only varied to escape the bogs, mountains, small ponds, water streams, &c., of which we met with many. This was the third day we had been in search of the Chaudiere, who were only seven computed miles distant the 28th inst. Nor were we possessed of any certainty that our course would bring us either to the lake or river, not knowing the point it lay from where we started. However, we came to a resolution to continue it. In this state of uncertainty, we wandered through hideous swamps and mountainous precipices, with the conjoint addition of cold, wet and hunger, not to mention our fatigue—with the terrible apprehension of famishing in this desert. The pretended pilot was not less frightened than many of the rest; added to that the severe execrations he received, from the front of the army to the rear, made his office not a little disagreeable. Several of the men towards evening were ready to give up any thoughts of ever arriving at the desired haven. Hunger and fatigue had so much the ascendency over many of the poor fellows, added to their despair of arrival, that some of them were left in the river, nor were heard of afterwards. In turn with Col. Greene, I carried the compass the greater part of this day. In this condition, we proceeded with as little knowledge of where we were, or where we should get to, as if we had been in the unknown interior of Africa, or the deserts of Arabia. Just as the sun was departing, we brought a pond or lake, which finally proved to be Chaudiere, and soon the small foot-path made by the other division of the army, whose choice turned to their account. Our arrival here was succeeded with three huzzas, and then came to our encampment.

Tuesday, 31st.—The appearance of daylight roused us as usual, and we had advanced with all possible speed till about 11 o'clock, ere we saw the Chandiere river, which we last night imagined within a mile. Animated afresh with the sight of a stream, which we very well knew would conduct us into the inhabitants if our strength continued, we proceeded with renewed vigor. The emptying of the Chaudiere is beautiful, and formed a very agreeable ascent, though the stream is somewhat rapid. The land was now much descending, yet very difficult travelling. The spruce, cedar and hemlock were the chief growth of the earth, and these were in tolerable plenty, almost impenetrably so in many places. We now began to discover the wrecked batteaux of those who conducted the ammunition, &c. These were seven in number, who followed the seven mile stream into the Chaudiere lake, river, &c., and soon came to an encampment, where I found Capt. Morgan and most of the boatmen who were wrecked upon a fall in the river, losing everything except their lives, which they all saved by swimming, except one of Morgan's riflemen. This was the first man drowned in all the dangers we were exposed to, and the third [lost] by casualties, except some lost in the wilderness, the number unknown. At this encampment was Lieut. McCleland, of Morgan's company, almost expiring with a violent *peripneumonia*. Necessaries were distributed as much as possible, with two lads of the company in charge of him. Nor was this poor fellow the only one left sick upon this river. Life depending upon a vigorous push for the inhabitants, and that did not admit of any stay for any person; nor could the two lads have been prevailed upon had not provisions been dealt out sufficient to conduct them to the inhabitants, with the promising to send them relief as soon as possible from the settlements. In this general wreck, my medicine box suffered the fate of the rest, with a set of capital instruments, &c. Though little was to be feared from either my chirurgical apparatus or physical potions, I had, however, a few necessaries in that way in my knapsack, &c., with a lancet in my pocket, which enabled me at least to comply with the Sangradoine method.

On the 8th of November, Dr. Senter reached Point Levi, and soon after crossed the river with the army, which advanced to the Plains of Abraham, and on the 18th fell back to Point Aux-Trembles, to await the arrival of General Montgomery. When the army advanced to Quebec, and an assault upon the city had been planned, Dr. Senter solicited Colonel Arnold for permission to lead a company whose Captain was absent, and which, on that account, it was supposed would tarry behind. To this application, the following answer was returned:

"DEAR SIR,—I am much obliged to you for your offer, and glad to see you so spirited, but cannot consent you should take up arms, as you will be wanted in the way of your profession. You will please to prepare dressings, &c., and repair to the main guard house at 2 o'clock in the morning, with an assistant.

I am in haste, yours,

B. ARNOLD, Col.

Dr. Senter,
27 Dec., 1775."

Though disappointed in his patriotic purpose, the Doctor found ample scope for his services in the hospital, and singularly enough, the first subject of his professional skill was Colonel Arnold himself.

The small pox, which early appeared in the army, still extensively prevailed, and after the army fell back to Sorel, Dr. Senter was ordered by General Thomas to Montreal, to erect a Hospital for the reception of patients. On applying to General Arnold, he obtained a fine capacious house belonging to the East India Company, capable of accommodating about six hundred persons. The only precautionary measure known at that time was innoculation, which had not as yet become popular. Dr. Senter, for personal safety and perhaps as an example to the men, had already had the varioloid matter transferred into his arm, and innoculation became general. An entire regiment at a class went through the operation together, and had the disease so mildly that they were able to do garrison duty during the whole time.

On retiring from the army, in 1779, Dr. Senter established himself as a physician in the town of Cranston, R. I. About this time he was elected a Representative to the General Assembly from that town, and afterwards was appointed Surgeon and Physician General of the State. Subsequently he removed to Newport, where he continued the practice of his profession under the most favorable circumstances, as almost all the old physicians had either died or emigrated during the war. He became eminent not only as an industrious and successful practitioner, but also as the author of several essays on professional subjects, which appeared in the medical publications of the day, and added greatly to his reputation at home and in Europe. He was elected an honorary member of the Medical and Chirurgical Societies of Edinburg and London, and an honorary member of the Massachusetts Medical Society. Among his pupils were Dr. Danforth, "the Medical Hercules" of Boston, and Dr. Waterhouse, the accomplished botanist, professor and writer, and who introduced vaccination into America.

Dr. Senter married Eliza Arnold, daughter of Captain Rhodes Arnold, of Pawtuxet, R. I. He had four sons and two daughters. The eldest son, Horace Gates, was a physician of eminence, and was for some time in the Hospitals of London. His second son, Nathaniel Greene, was several years in the East India Service. His third son was Edward Gibson, also a student of medicine. His fourth son, Charles Churchill, died at the age of 17 years. His eldest daughter, Eliza Antoinette, married Rev. Nathan Bourne Crocker, D.D., for more than half a century the honored Rector of St. John's Church, in the City of Providence. His second daughter, Sarah Ann, married Clement S. Hunt, of the U. S. Navy.

For several years Dr. Senter was President of the Society of Cincinnati of Rhode Island. In person he was tall and well proportioned, and possessing great muscular strength. In his manners he was bland, dignified, and social. The late Rev. Dr. William Ellery Channing mentions him as "a physician of extensive practice, who was thought to unite with great experience a rare genius in his profession, and whose commanding figure rises before me at the distance of forty-five years, as a specimen of manly beauty, worthy the chisel of a Grecian sculptor." In the height of his reputation and usefulness, he was attacked with a disorder, caused by the severity of his professional labors, which terminated his life, to the great regret of his fellow-citizens, on the 21st day of December, 1799, at the age of forty-six years. His Journal of the Expedition against Quebec, which has been freely used in the preceding pages, was published by the Pennsylvania Historical Society in 1846, and is one of the most valuable memorials of the scenes it records.

Simeon Thayer, son of David and Jane Keith Thayer, was born in Mendon, Mass., April 30, 1737. His brothers and sisters were Jean, David, Susanna, George, Faithful, Jemima, Mary and Elizabeth. David Thayer, the father, was the grandson of Ferdinando, the son of

Thomas, who came early to New England with Margery his wife. Ferdinando married Huldah Hayward, of Braintree, Mass., Jan. 14, 1652. He lived in that town until after his father's decease, when he removed to Mendon with a Colony from Braintree and Weymouth.

Simeon, the subject of this notice, was apprenticed to a Peruke-maker, probably in Providence. His bold and decided nature loved adventure, and it is not surprising that we find him, in 1756, a member of a Rhode Island regiment, serving in the French War. In 1757, he served in the Massachusetts line, under the command of Col. Fry, and was principally in the Rangers, under Rogers. He was personally in three engagements with the Indians, in each of which many of the Rangers were killed. In August of the same year, he was in Fort William Henry, when taken by Montcalm, which surrendered on the morning of the 7th day from the commencement of the siege. After being detained twenty hours he, with the rest of the garrison, was disarmed and stripped of all his clothes, leaving him with only an under waistcoat. As he was passing down the road near Bloody Pond, he was attacked by an Indian, who seized him by the back of his waistcoat collar with the right hand and dragged him towards a swamp on the left, about twelve or fifteen rods. His captor held in his left hand a tomahawk and scalping knife. Thayer's shoulder, as the Indian was forcing him along, struck against a small tree, which stopped him. His waistcoat broke open and slipped off, which, as the Indian was pulling with main strength, precipitated him upon the earth, at some distance. Thayer being thus disengaged, ran into the woods, where he joined the rest of the troops. In passing on, the road being crowded, he with a companion took a path called the plank guard path. They soon perceived an Indian with a tomahawk pursuing them. They both ran, and coming to a tree that had been blown up by the roots, he crept under, while his companion, endeavoring to leap over, was struck by the tomahawk, thrown with unerring skill, and was killed. Thayer made his escape once more, by running round the top of the tree, and in an hour or two reached Fort Edward. The excessive fatigue of running so great a distance in a short time, in intensely hot weather, brought on an inflammation which impaired his health for many years, and prevented his entering the service again during the war.*

*Captain JONATHAN CARVER, a native of Connecticut, and who commanded a company of Provincial troops in the "French war," was at Fort William Henry as a volunteer during this siege, and thus describes the scenes that followed the capitulation:

"In consideration of the gallant defence the garrison had made, they were to be permitted to march out with all the honors of war, to be allowed covered waggons

On returning to Providence, young Thayer probably settled down in the business to which he had been bred, as the registry of deeds shows that in 1761, "Simeon Thayer, Periwig-maker," purchased an estate on "Stamper's Hill," of Margaret Smith, weaver, for £2100, "old tenor." The same year he was married. The events that transpired between this date and the first resistance to British tyranny, on the waters of Rhode Island in 1772, were well calculated to raise the blood of Thayer to a fever-heat of patriotism, and prepare him for the step he subsequently took. When the design of Britain made it necessary for the Colonies to arm for their defence, he was an officer in a chartered company of Grenadiers in Providence. His zeal for the public welfare and the reputation he had acquired as a friend to liberty,

---

to transport their baggage to Fort Edward, and a guard to protect them from the fury of the savages.

The morning after the capitulation was signed, as soon as day broke, the whole garrison, now consisting of about two thousand men, besides women and children, were drawn up within the lines, and on the point of marching off, when great numbers of the Indians gathered about, and began to plunder. We were at first in hopes that this was their only view, and suffered them to proceed without opposition. Indeed it was not in our power to make any, had we been so inclined; for though we were permitted to carry off our arms, yet we were not allowed a single round of ammunition. In these hopes however we were disappointed; for presently some of them began to attack the sick and wounded, when such as were not able to crawl into the ranks, notwithstanding they endeavored to avert the fury of their enemies by their shrieks or groans, were soon dispatched.

Here we were fully in expectation that the disturbance would have concluded, and our little army began to move; but in a short time we saw the front division driven back, and discovered that we were entirely encircled by the savages. We expected every moment that the guard, which the French by the articles of capitulation, had agreed to allow us, would have arrived, and put an end to our apprehensions; but none appeared. The Indians now began to strip every one without exception of their arms and clothes, and those who made the least resistance felt the weight of their tomahawks.

I happened to be in the rear division, but it was not long before I shared the fate of my companions. Three or four of the savages laid hold of me, and whilst some held their weapons over my head, the others soon disrobed me of my coat, waistcoat, hat and buckles, omitting not to take from me what money I had in my pocket. As this was transacted close by the passage that led from the lines on to the plain, near which a French sentinel was posted, I ran to him and claimed his protection; but he only called me an English dog, and thrust me with violence back again into the midst of the Indians.

I now endeavored to join a body of our troops that were crowded together at some distance; but innumerable were the blows that were made at me with different weapons as I passed on; luckily however the savages were so close together that they could not strike at me without endangering each other. Notwithstanding which one of them found means to make a thrust at me with a spear, which grazed my side, and from another I received a wound, with the same kind of weapon, in my ancle. At length I gained the spot where my countrymen stood, and forced

pointed him out as a suitable person to be trusted, and in May, 1775, he was accordingly appointed a Captain by the General Assembly. Three days after his appointment, he had completed his company, having enlisted every man himself. On Sunday, the 19th of May, an express arrived from near Boston, stating that the British were marching out to Dorchester, to burn some buildings. In two hours' time, Thayer assembled his company, dealt out their arms, ammunition, blankets, &c., and marched with every man. He was met nine miles from town by an express, and informed that the British had returned into Boston, and as it was then late, he halted and took up his quarters in Attleborough meeting house for that night. The next day he proceeded on to Roxbury, where he arrived eight days before any other

---

myself into the midst of them. But before I got thus far out of the hands of the Indians, the collar and wristbands of my shirt were all that remained of it, and my flesh was scratched and torn in many places by their savage gripes.

By this time the war whoop was given, and the Indians began to murder those that were nearest to them without distinction. It is not in the power of words to give any tolerable idea of the horrid scene that now ensued; men, women and children were dispatched in the most wanton and cruel manner, and immediately scalped. Many of these savages drank the blood of their victims, as it flowed warm from the fatal wound.

We now perceived, though too late to avail us, that we were to expect no relief from the French; and that, contrary to the agreement they had so lately signed to allow us a sufficient force to protect us from these insults, they tacitly permitted them; for I could plainly perceive the French officers walking about at some distance, discoursing together with apparent unconcern. For the honor of human nature I would hope that this flagrant breach of every sacred law proceeded rather from the savage disposition of the Indians, which I acknowledge it is sometimes almost impossible to control, and which might now unexpectedly have arrived to a pitch not easily to be restrained, than to any premeditated design in the French commander. An unprejudiced observer would, however, be apt to conclude, that a body of ten thousand troops, mostly christian troops, had it in their power to prevent the massacre from becoming so general. But whatever was the cause from which it arose, the consequences of it were dreadful, and not to be paralleled in modern history.

As the circle in which I stood enclosed by this time was much thinned, and death seemed to be approaching with hasty strides, it was proposed by some of the most resolute to make one vigorous effort, and endeavor to force our way through the savages, the only probable method of preserving our lives that now remained. This, however desperate, was resolved on, and about twenty of us sprung at once into the midst of them.

In a moment we were all separated, and what was the fate of my companions I could not learn till some months after, when I found that only six or seven of them effected their design. Intent only on my own hazardous situation, I endeavored to make my way through my savage enemies in the best manner possible. And I have often been astonished since, when I have recollected with what composure I took, as I did, every necessary step for my preservation. Some I overturned, being at that time young and athletic, and others I passed by, dexterously avoiding their

troops from Rhode Island. On the 20th of September he was chosen to accompany Arnold in his memorable march by the way of the Kennebec river to Quebec, and in the unsuccessful attack on the town was, with many other officers and soldiers, made prisoner. He was kept closely confined for nine months, part of that time in irons, on board a prison ship, before he was admitted to parole. In September, 1776, he returned to Providence.

On the 1st of July, 1777, Captain Thayer was exchanged, and in the same month the General Assembly of Rhode Island ordered a "genteel silver hilted sword" to be presented to him as a testimony of their sense of his services. In anticipation of his exchange, the General Assembly had, in February preceding, appointed him Major in one

---

weapons; till at last two very stout chiefs, of the most savage tribes, as I could distinguish by their dress, whose strength I could not resist, laid hold of me by each arm, and began to force me through the crowd.

I now resigned myself to my fate, not doubting but that they intended to dispatch me, and then to satiate their vengeance with my blood, as I found they were hurrying me towards a retired swamp that lay at some distance. But before we had got many yards, an English gentleman of some distinction, as I could discover by his breeches, the only covering he had on, which were of fine scarlet velvet, rushed close by us. One of the Indians instantly relinquished his hold, and springing on this new object, endeavored to seize him as his prey; but the gentleman being strong, threw him on the ground, and would probably have got away, had not he who held my other arm, quitted me to assist his brother. I seized the opportunity, and hastened away to join another party of English troops that were yet unbroken, and stood in a body at some distance. But before I had taken many steps, I hastily cast my eye towards the gentleman, and saw the Indian's tomahawk gash into his back and heard him utter his last groan; this added both to my speed and desperation.

I had left this shocking scene but a few yards, when a fine boy about twelve years of age, that had hitherto escaped, came up to me, and begged that I would let him lay hold of me, so that he might stand some chance of getting out of the hands of the savages. I told him that I would give him every assistance in my power, and to this purpose bid him lay hold; but in a few moments he was torn from my side, and by his shrieks I judge was soon demolished. I could not help forgetting my own cares for a minute, to lament the fate of so young a sufferer; but it was utterly impossible for me to take any methods to prevent it.

I now got once more into the midst of friends, but we were unable to afford each other any succor. As this was the division that had advanced the farthest from the fort, I thought there might be a possibility (though but a bare one) of my forcing my way through the outer ranks of the Indians, and getting to a neighboring wood, which I perceived at some distance. I was still encouraged to hope by the almost miraculous preservation I had already experienced.

Nor were my hopes in vain, or the efforts I made ineffectual. Suffice it to say, that I reached the wood; but by the time I had penetrated a little way into it, my breath was so exhausted that I threw myself into a brake, and lay for some minutes apparently at the last gasp. At length I recovered the power of respiration; but my apprehensions returned with all their former force, when I saw several savages

of the Rhode Island regiments, and as soon as circumstances permitted, he joined the army and marched to Red Bank. Here he was detached with 150 men to join Colonel Samuel Smith, then in command of Fort Mifflin, built on the lower end of Mud Island in the Delaware, to prevent the passage of the enemy's vessels up the river. He continued there three days, until the Hessians appeared as if they intended an attack on Red Bank, when he received an express from Col. Greene, ordering him to return with his troops, which he immediately did, and reached the fort just as the Hessians appeared in sight. Major Thayer commanded according to his rank during the action, and was detached about the dusk of the evening, with a small force to bring in the wounded. As he was employed in this humane service, two Hessian grenadiers approached and told him that their commanding officer, Count Donop, was lying wounded in the edge of the woods, near where their artillery played. Suspecting an attempt to decoy him into an ambuscade, he placed them under guard, telling them if they deceived him, they would immediately be put to death; to this they readily assented, and conducted him to the place where they found the Count lying under a tree mortally wounded. The Count asked the Major if he was an officer, and of what rank, of which being satisfied he surrendered himself a prisoner. Major Thayer caused six men to take him in a blanket and carry him with all possible care to the fort, where he was received by Col. Greene.

Colonel Smith commanded on Mud Island from the latter part of September, with the exception of a few days, until the 11th of November, when, being wounded and worn down with fatigue, his request to retire from the fort was granted. The command then devolved upon

---

pass by, probably in pursuit of me, at no very great distance. In this situation I knew not whether it was better to proceed, or endeavor to conceal myself where I lay, till night came on; fearing, however, that they would return the same way, I thought it most prudent to get further from the dreadful scene of my distresses. Accordingly, striking into another part of the wood, I hastened on as fast as the briars and the loss of one of my shoes would permit me; and after a slow progress of some hours, gained a hill that overlooked the plain which I had just left, from whence I could discern that the bloody storm still raged with unabated fury.

But not to tire my readers, I shall only add, that after passing three days without subsistence, and enduring the severity of the cold dews for three nights, I at length reached Fort Edward; where with proper care my body soon recovered its wonted strength, and my mind, as far as the recollection of the late melancholy events would permit, its usual composure.

It was computed that fifteen hundred persons were killed or made prisoners by these savages during this fatal day. Many of the latter were carried off by them and never returned. A few, through favorable accidents, found their way back to their native country, after having experienced a long and severe captivity."

Lieutenant Colonel Russell, of the Connecticut line, an amiable, sensible man, and an excellent officer, but being exhausted by fatigue, and broken down in health, he requested to be recalled. The Commander-in-Chief, his Excellency General Washington, had no idea of holding the place through the campaign, but wished to retard the operations of the enemy until the main army should be re-inforced by the Massachusetts brigade, marching from the conquest of Saratoga, when he would be in sufficient force to cover the country, or to meet the enemy's whole force in the field. Upon the 12th of November, he signified his orders to the commanding General, at Woodberry, on the Jersey side, who had the direction of all the forces below Philadelphia, to defend the island as long as possible without sacrificing the garrison. To defend it was absolutely impossible, unless the siege could be raised by an attack upon the besiegers from the main army. This was deemed impracticable by a general council of war, and therefore not farther considered as an ultimate object. Nothing could then present itself to a relieving officer, fully informed of all the circumstances, but certain death, or an improbable escape, without the possibility of contending upon equal terms. The love of our country may lead us to the field of battle, ambition may lure us to particular enterprises, but magnanimity alone can soar above every danger! The commanding General could not detach an officer in rotation; his reasons were insuperable. In a moment so critical, when everything dear to his feelings required an immediate decision, happy for him, and more happy for the United States, Major Thayer presented himself as a volunteer! The offer was accepted with inexpressible satisfaction; and from the 12th to the morning of the 16th of November, he defended the Island with the greatest address, against a furious and almost continued cannonade and bombardment from a variety of batteries at small distances. The defences at best were trifling; the place itself was ill chosen. Hog Island and Billingspost instead of Mud Island and Red Bank. But on the morning of the 15th, the whole British force was displayed from their land batteries and their shipping in the river. The small garrison sustained and repelled the shock with astonishing intrepidity, for several hours, assisted from our galleys and batteries on the Jersey shore. By the middle of the day, these defences were leveled with the common mud, and the gallant officers and men philosophically expected each other's fate in the midst of carnage.

The grenadiers and light infantry of the British were paraded on the opposite shore, and the Vigilant, an Indiaman, cut down to a battery of twenty twenty-four pounders on one side, lay within twenty yards of the troops. The attack was incessant. Two attempts from our galleys were unsuccessfully made to board the Vigilant. The commanding General was determined to fight the enemy on the Island if the Vigilant could be taken. She could not; and nothing remained but to secure the garrison, whose distance from the enemy on both sides was not half so far as from the body of his troops upon the shore. During this day more than one thousand and thirty discharges of cannon from twelve and thirty-two pounders were made in twenty minutes. Such a day America never saw till then! Early in the evening of the 15th, Major Thayer dispatched all his garrison, less than three hundred in number, to the shore, excepting forty, with whom he remained, braving death itself. At twelve at night, between the 15th and 16th, the barracks were fired, all the military stores having previously been sent away, and the Major and his brave companions, he being the last from the scene of slaughter, arrived at Red Bank, to the joy and astonishment of all the army.*

The first principal battle in 1778 was fought by Washington at Monmouth, N. J., June 28, a day of intense heat, and made memorable by the reprimand of Lee and the gallant conduct of Mary Pitcher, the wife of an American artillery-man, whose place she took when he fell wounded. In this battle Major Thayer participated, being then under Col. Sylla. He was detached with Gen. Scott to watch the motions of the enemy, and on the evening before the action the detachment of Scott was ordered to join the army. In this battle, Major Thayer underwent great fatigue. Sylla's regiment, by particular leave of General Washington, marched to attack the enemy, who appeared on the left of the American army, and drove them through a morass. In this movement, the Major experienced in his head a wind-concussion, by the near passage of a cannon ball, which caused the blood to gush from both his eyes. Rallying from the shock, he tied a handkerchief over his face, and continued at his post all night. The effect of the concussion was to destroy his right eye. The next day he joined his Brigade, and being in excessive pain, he obtained leave to return to Morristown until he should recover.

*General Knox, writing to Colonel Lamb, says, "The defence of Fort Mifflin was as gallant as is to be found in history. . . . . The brave little garrison, then commanded by Major Thayer, of the Rhode Island troops, had but two cannon but what were dismounted. These soon shared the fate of the others. Every body who appeared on the platform was killed or wounded, by the musketry from the tops of the ships, whose yards almost hung over the battery. Long before night there was not a single palisade left. All the embrasures ruined, and the whole parapet levelled. All the block houses had been battered down some days before."

Major Thayer remained at Morristown five weeks before he so far recovered as to be able to attend to duty. In the mean time, his regiment had been ordered to Rhode Island, to support Gen. Sullivan. Thither he followed, hoping to be in season to render service, and arrived three days before the General retreated from the Island.

During the year 1779, Major Thayer was actively engaged in superintending enlistments, and in other ways promoting the interests of the Continental army. In December of that year he went by order of the General Assembly to headquarters in New Jersey, to transact business for the State. For the expenses of this journey £200 were provided, and also a horse for the orderly who accompanied him. In 1780, he was Major in Colonel Angell's regiment in New Jersey. At Springfield the regiment was stationed at the bridge, when the enemy attacked that place. On that occasion he was posted in the centre, with orders to watch the motions of the enemy, and give intelligence to the commander of each wing. This post he sustained under four different attacks, and passed the road in front and escaped four different times during the heavy fire, within pistol shot. When the regiment was forced to quit the ground Major Thayer commanded the rear, was the last to leave the field, and joined Gen. Greene on Rocky Hill. After the enemy retreated, Gen. Stark, who then commanded the brigade to which the Major belonged, requested that he would follow the enemy's rear, and make what discoveries he could of their motions. This request he complied with, and followed alone on horseback, keeping in sight of them until they crossed Elizabethtown bridge, notwithstanding whole platoons fired at him. The results of his observations he reported to Generals Greene and Stark. When the Marquis, de Lafayette was in danger of being surprised at Barren Hill Church, Major Thayer was chosen by him with 300 men to cover his retreat, where there was scarcely a possibility of escaping either being killed or taken prisoner. Fortunately, however, the Major succeeded in bringing off the whole of his detachment in the face of the enemy,—the Marquis having moved off the main body some time before.

The brilliant defence of Fort Mifflin by Major Thayer was the theme of universal praise. Congress, not aware that Colonel Smith had retired from the command previous to the battle, and prompt to acknowledge brave conduct, passed a complimentary resolution directing an elegant sword to be presented to the Colonel as a token of their high sense of his merit in that affair. The discovery of the error was too late for it to be corrected, and Colonel Smith accepted the sword as the reward of a battle he did not fight! The unintentional injustice of

Congress was keenly felt both by Major Thayer and his friends in Rhode Island. General Varnum and Colonel Angell, his military compatriots, and the late venerable John Howland, Esq., a soldier of the Revolution, set the subject right before the public, in communications that were published in the Providence Gazette in 1786, and in the Providence Journal in 1840, and all of which are preserved in Judge Cowell's "Spirit of '76." But while the page of history has been corrected, the official injustice is perpetuated.

By the act of Congress of Oct. 3, 1780, the two Continental regiments of Rhode Island were consolidated, to take effect Jan. 1, 1781. Under this arrangement Major Thayer retired from the service. He was subsequently for three successive years chosen by the General Assembly Brigadier General of the Militia of Providence County.

General Thayer was of medium height, active and energetic in his business habits, and in private intercourse an agreeable companion. He was married three times, viz:

1. To Huldah Jackson, daughter of Stephen Jackson, Esq., of Providence. She was born Nov. —, 1738, and died April 28, 1771.

2. To Mrs. Mary Tourtelott, born Dec. 24, 1742.

3. To Mrs. —— Angell, sister to Huldah, his first wife. After the death of General Thayer, she married Darius Daniels. She was born in 1763, and died March 10, 1803, aged 40 years.

The children of General Thayer were

Nancy, born March 7, 1762; died May 1, 1783.
William Tourtelott, born May 11, 1767.
Susan, born April 24, 1768; died same date.
Stephen Tourtelott, died Feb. 25, 1769.
Hannah Tourtelott, born Jan. 1, 1769; died March 31, 1769.
Simeon, born March 24, 1770; died Sept. 9, 1791.
Polly, born Oct. 25, 1772; died May 28, 1814.
Richard Montgomery, born Dec. 3, 1775.
Henry, born April 10, 1785.

After leaving the army Major Thayer purchased, in 1781, of Nathaniel Balch, hatter, an estate consisting of a house and lot situated on "Stamper's Hill" for "$1350 Spanish milled dollars," and also a lot in the same vicinity, of Enos Smith, of Killingly, Ct., for "£10, lawful money." He erected a dwelling house on the spot now a small park near the head of Constitution Hill, and in 1784 opened a public house known as the "Montgomery Hotel," which he kept for several years, when he sold out and purchased a farm in Cumberland. There he continued to reside until his decease, which occurred Tuesday, Oct. 14th, 1800, in the 63d year of his age. He died by casualty, having fallen or been thrown from his horse into a brook, while riding home from Providence, and being killed by the concussion or drowned. On Thursday, Oct. 16th, his remains were interred in the North burial ground, in Providence. The Society of Cincinnati, of which General Thayer died a member, voted to wear the usual badge of mourning on the left arm for twenty-one days, as a testimony of respect.*

Major General JOHN THOMAS was descended from a respectable family in Plymouth County, Mass., and served with reputation in the war of 1756 against the French and Indians. In April, 1775, he resided in Kingston, Mass., and raised a regiment for the Continental service, and marched to Cambridge. He was soon appointed by Congress a Brigadier General, and during the siege of Boston commanded a division of the provincial troops at Roxbury. In March, 1776, he was appointed Major General, and after the death of Montgomery was entrusted with the command of the army in Canada. As stated in the Introduction to this Journal, he fell back with his forces from before Quebec to Sorel, was there taken sick of small pox and conveyed to Chambly, where he died May 30, 1776. Gen. Thomas was a man of sound judgment and undoubted courage. He was beloved by his soldiers, and in private life endeared to friends by the amiability of his character.

Captain JOHN TOPHAM was a native of Newport, R. I. His early history is unknown. When the first measures were adopted for resisting the oppressive acts of the British government, he was found acting with the friends of freedom. He was appointed Captain-Lieutenant of Major Forrester's company of the regiment of Newport and Bristol, commanded by Colonel Thomas Church, forming a part of the "Army of Observation" raised by the General Assembly of Rhode Island in May, 1775. It is said, that on hearing the news of the battle of Lexington, Captain Topham raised a company and marched to Cambridge.

---

*CAPTAIN THAYER'S PAROLE.

I, Simeon Thayre, of Providence,

In the Province of Rhode Island, hereby pledge my Faith and word of Honor to General Carleton, that I shall not do or say any thing contrary to the Interest of His Majesty, or his Government, and that whenever required to do so, I shall repair to whatever Place his Excellency, or any other His Majesty's Commanders-in-Chief in America, shall judge expedient to order me.

Given under my Hand at Quebec,

this 3d Day of August, 1776.

SIMEON THAYRE.

A true copy.

There he joined the Continental army under Washington, then holding Boston in siege. He was subsequently assigned to Colonel Arnold's detachment for service in Canada. Of the sufferings of himself and of his men in their march through the wilderness, his Journal (though imperfect) still preserved, is an interesting evidence. He was among the officers who, when the prospect of starvation was before them, unhesitatingly voted in a council of war to proceed. In the assault upon Quebec he made a noble record for bravery and efficiency. Here he was taken prisoner, and for four months and twelve days was not permitted to set his feet on the ground. But this close confinement only served to enhance the value of the freedom to secure which he had perilled his life, and he panted for an early opportunity to prove his unabated devotion.

While still a prisoner, and in prospect of his early release, Captain Topham was among the officers recommended by Washington (Oct. 12, 1776,) to command a company in one of the two new regiments then about to be raised in Rhode Island. Writing to Governor Cooke on this subject, Washington says, "Too much regard cannot be had to the choosing of men of merit, and such as are not only under the influence of a warm attachment to their country, but who also possess sentiments of principles of the strictest honor." He adds: "In respect to the officers that were in the Canada expedition, their behavior and merit, and the severities they have experienced, entitle them to a particular notice, in my opinion. However, as they are under their paroles, I would recommend that vacancies should be reserved for such as you think fit to promote, not wishing them to accept commissions immediately, or to do the least act that may be interpreted a violation of their engagement."

After being exchanged, the General Assembly of Rhode Island, in February, 1777, chose Captain Topham a Captain in the first Continental battalion, under Major Ward. In June following, he was chosen Lieutenant Colonel in the brigade raised for fifteen months, under Colonel Archibald Crary. In December of the same year, he held the same rank in the second battalion of the regiment of artillery, under Colonel William Barton. In February, 1778, he was chosen Colonel in place of Colonel Barton, who had been transferred to the Continental service, and held the position until the brigade was disbanded. In February, 1779, he was made Colonel of the second battalion of Infantry. In June of the same year the two battalions were consolidated under him; and in 1780 he received the thanks of the General Assembly for the great fidelity and ability with which he had discharged his military duties. After the war, Colonel Topham engaged in mercantile pursuits. In 1780, he was elected a Deputy to the General Assembly from Newport. He was again elected in 1783, 1784 to 1788, and again in 1791 and 1792. He was a useful member of the Assembly. Colonel Topham died in Newport, September 26th, 1793, in the 55th year of his age. On Sunday afternoon, the 29th, his remains, preceded by the ancient and honorable fraternity of Masons, of which he was a member, and followed by his relatives, friends, and a large concourse of citizens, were committed to the grave.

Captain OLIVER HANCHET, son of John 3d and Mary Sheldon Hanchet, was born in Suffield, Conn., August 7th, 1741. Of his boy life little is known. May 29th, 1766, he married Rachel Gillet. In the commencement of the Revolutionary war, he commanded a company of Provincials and marched to Cambridge, where he was assigned to Arnold's expedition. In his march through the wilderness, Capt. Hanchet was mostly with the advance, engaged in opening the way for the main body of the army, and performing such other services as were essential to its rapid march. After reaching Dead River, he set out with fifty men for Chaudiere lake, to forward provisions from the French inhabitants of Sartigan, for the use of the army. Subseqently, in leaving the army (who took water conveyance on Chaudiere lake) to go on by land, he mistook his course, and with sixty men was led into low ground overflowed by water, through which they waded up to their waists for the distance of two miles, when they were discovered by Col. Arnold, who sent batteaux to relieve them from their uncomfortable situation. The trials and perils of the rest of the march to Point Levi were shared in common with the army. At Quebec Captain Hanchet was taken prisoner, and held with other officers until paroles were granted in August, 1776. He appears not to have entertained a favorable opinion of Arnold, and was numbered among the disaffected towards him. Of his life after being exchanged, no particulars have been obtained. He died May 26th, 1816, aged 75 years. His widow died March 28th, 1821. Both were buried in the West Parish of Suffield.

Lieutenant JAMES WEBB, of Newport, R. I., was among the officers recommended to consideration by Washington, for meritorious conduct, and was chosen first Lieutenant in the Continental battalion, by the General Assembly of Rhode Island, in February, 1777.

Captain SAMUEL WARD was born at Westerly, Rhode Island, on the 17th of Nov., 1756, and was the son of Samuel Ward, Governor of that State, and Anne Ray, daughter of Simon Ray and Deborah Greene, a relative of General Nathanael Greene.* His father, and indeed all his family connexions, were ardent supporters of the Revolution, and, from the first collision between Great Britain and her colonies, advocates of the independence of the United States, an event which his father predicted as inevitable, as early as 1766.

Capt. Ward was educated at Brown University in Providence, and was a classmate of Solomon Drowne, subsequently the distinguished Professor of Botany in that institution. Hostilities commencing about the time he left college, he joined the Rhode Island army of observation,

---

*SAMUEL WARD, father of Capt. Samuel, was born at Newport, Rhode Island, May 27th, 1725. He was the son of Richard Ward, who was Governor of Rhode Island in 1741 and 1742, and the grandson of Thomas Ward, who came to this country in the times of Charles II, and who died in Rhode Island in 1689, a highly esteemed and respectable citizen.

Samuel was educated at the excellent classical schools in Newport, R. I. He married Anne Ray, of Block Island, and settled in Westerly. He represented that town in the General Assembly of Rhode Island for several years, and was a delegate from the Colony to a convention held at Hartford, during the French war, to consult with Lord Loudon, as to the best course to be pursued in prosecuting the war. Mr. Ward was chosen Governor of Rhode Island in 1762, and again in 1765, and continued in office until 1767. He early took ground against the encroachments of the Mother Country on Colonial rights. He denounced the stamp act and the tax on tea, and was elected delegate to the Continental Congress, in which he acted a conspicuous part. He early foresaw the separation of the Colonies from Great Britain, and in a letter to his son, said: "These Colonies are destined to an early independence, and you will live to see my words verified"—a prophecy ten years later fulfilled.

While the Congress was in Committee of the whole on the consideration of the state of America, Mr. Ward occupied the chair. He was chairman of a committee which originated a resolution, "that a General be appointed to command all the Continental forces raised, or to be raised, for the defence of American liberty." When, under this resolution, Congress proceeded to ballot, Gov. Ward gave his vote for General Washington, to whom, through life, he remained devotedly attached. His feelings throughout the contest are nobly expressed in a letter to his brother, written in 1775: "No man living, perhaps, is more fond of his children than I am, and I am not so old as to be tired of life; and yet, as far as I can now judge, the tenderest connexions and the most important private concerns, are very minute objects. Heaven save my country, I was going to say, is my first, my last, and almost my only prayer."

Governor Ward strongly advocated the Declaration of Independence, but did not live to affix his signature to that immortal instrument. He died in Philadelphia of small pox, March 26th, 1776, in the fifty-first year of his age. His remains were exhumed in 1860, and brought to Rhode Island. The slab erected by the State over his grave bears testimony to his great abilities, his unshaken integrity, his ardor in the cause of freedom, and his fidelity in the offices he filled.

in which he was appointed a Captain on the 8th of May, 1775. The army was raised in the name of His Majesty George III, for the preservation of His Majesty's loyal and faithful subjects of the Colony of Rhode Island. His commission, which was given by his uncle, Henry Ward, the Secretary of Rhode Island, (the Governor and Lieut. Governor being Tories,) authorized him 'in case of an invasion or assault of a common enemy, to infest or disturb this or any other of His Majesty's Colonies in America, to alarm and gather together the company under your command,' 'and therewith to the utmost of your skill and ability, you are to resist, expel, kill and destroy them, in order to preserve the interest of His Majesty and his good subjects in these parts.' Like their brethren the covenanters—

'Who swore at first to fight
For the King's safety and his right,
And after marched to find him out
And charged him home with horse and foot,'

the Whigs of the Revolution found no inconsistency in availing themselves of the authority of the King as the constitutional head of the government, to preserve and maintain their constitutional rights. In the month of May, 1775, the father and son both left their home—the one to represent the Colony in the Continental Congress, and the other to defend her liberties in the field. Capt. Ward joined the army besieging Boston — burning with a vehement desire to vindicate the rights of the Colonies. In one of his letters to his family, dated Prospect Hill, July 30, 1775, addressing his younger brothers, he says: "As you grow in stature, pray take pains to be manly: remember that you all may have an opportunity of standing forth to fight the battles of your country. This afternoon we expected to have had an engagement. We may have one to-night. The regulars are now landing in Charlestown from Boston. I thank God we are ready to meet them."

With such an ardent spirit, young Ward, then in the 19th year of his age, was not likely to hesitate in embracing an opportunity of advancing the cause he had espoused; nor was it long before one was presented. In September, 1775, Colonel Benedict Arnold, then one of the most enterprising of America's sons, (but afterwards 'quantum mutatus abillo Hectore!') was invested with the command of 1100 volunteers, destined to join Montgomery at Quebec, by way of the Kennebec river. The country was then an unexplored wilderness, and they were obliged to transport their provisions and munitions for the whole distance, where they did not follow the river, without the aid of animals. Even when ascending the river, the volunteers were compelled to drag the boats over the waterfalls and portages, and after leaving the river, the provisions and munitions, packed in small kegs, were placed on the backs of the soldiers and carried more than 300 miles, through thick and pathless woods, and over lofty mountains and deep morasses. So great were the difficulties, that a part of the detachment actually abandoned the expedition, and returned to Cambridge to avoid starvation. Capt. Ward, the youngest officer in the expedition, together with his company, persevered, and after unheard of privations arrived before Quebec in Nov., 1775. A letter from him on the 26th of that month to his family, dated at Point-aux-Trembles, gives a vivid account of the hardships of the expedition.

"It would take too much time to tell you what we have undergone. However, as a summary of the whole, we have gone up one of the most rapid rivers in the world, where the water was so shoal that, moderately speaking, we have waded 100 miles. We were thirty days in a wilderness that none but savages ever attempted to pass. We marched 100 miles upon short three days' provisions, waded over three rapid rivers, marched through snow and ice *barefoot*, passed over the St. Lawrence, where it was guarded by the enemy's frigates, and are now about twenty-four miles from the city to recruit our worn-out natures. Gen. Montgomery intends to join us immediately, so that we have a winter's campaign before us; but I trust we shall have the glory of taking Quebec!"

That hope, unhappily, was not realized. The attack upon that city failed, and Capt. Ward, with the principal part of his company, having penetrated under the command of Arnold, through the first barrier, was surrounded by a superior force and compelled to surrender. The following letter written by Governor Samuel Ward to his daughter, Miss Nancy Ward, afterwards Mrs. Anne, wife of Ephan Clarke, Esq., in relation to Captain Ward's capture, expresses the anxious interest of a parent, and presents in a favorable light the military conduct of the son:

Philadelphia, 21st Jan., 1776.

MY DEAREST:

Blessed be God, your dear brother, of whom I never heard one word, from the time he left Fort Weston until last Monday, is alive and well, and has behaved well. There is a gentleman here who saw him the day before the attack upon Quebec. He had been very ill with the yellow jaundice; but one Captain McLean, formerly of Boston, took him home and cured him.

This gentleman tells me he was happy to have gone upon that service. General Montgomery was killed in the attack, and his troops immediately retired, which left the whole force of the enemy to attack your kinsman, Lieut. Colonel Greene, who, upon Arnold's being wounded and carried off, led the detachment on nobly. They carried two barriers, attacked the third, and fought gloriously with much superior forces, under cover also. Four hours after, being overpowered by numbers, they were compelled to surrender prisoners of war, and are very kindly treated.

I have written by express to your brother, and shall send him some money. Call upon all who owe us for some. I shall want it much.

Write immediately to Colonel Greene's wife that he is well, and treated with great humanity. He has acquired vast honor in the service, and I doubt not will soon be exchanged. In the mean time, I have written Sammy to let him know his family is well, and that if he needs any money he can draw upon me.

Your affectionate father,

SAMUEL WARD.

P. S. In Colonel Greene's detachment there were 120 killed and wounded—nearly half killed. Troops begin their march from here to-morrow, to reïnforce our army in Canada.

While in captivity, Capt. Ward received the following letter from his father, which, from the excellence of its sentiments, and as fully illustrating the principles of the leading patriots of that time, is inserted at length.

Philadelphia, January 21st, 1776.

MY DEAR SON:—I most devoutly thank God that you are alive, in good health, and have behaved well. You have now a new scene of action—to behave well as a prisoner. You have been taught from your infancy the love of God, of all mankind, and of your country. In a due discharge of these various duties of life, consist true honor, religion and virtue. I hope no situation or trial, however severe, will tempt you to violate these sound, these immutable laws of God and nature. You will now have time for reflection. Improve it well; examine your own heart. Eradicate, as much as human frailty admits, the seeds of vice and folly. Correct your temper. Expand the benevolent feelings of your soul, and impress and establish the noble principles of private and public virtue so deeply in it, that your whole life may be directed by them. Next to these great and essential duties, improve your mind by the best authors you can borrow. Learn the French language, and be continually acquiring, as far as your situation admits, every useful accomplishment. Shun every species of debauchery and vice, as certain and inevitable ruin, here and hereafter. There is one vice, which, though often to be met with in polite company, I cannot but consider as unworthy of the gentleman as well as the Christian. I mean swearing. Avoid it at all times.

All ranks of people here have the highest sense of the great bravery and merit of Col. Arnold, and all his officers and men. Though prisoners they have acquired immortal honor. Proper attention will be paid to them. In the mean time, behave, my dear son, with great circumspection, prudence and firmness. Enter into no engagements inconsistent with your duty to your country. Such as you may make, keep inviolate with the strictest honor. Besides endeavoring to make yourself as easy and happy as possible in your present situation, you will pay the greatest attention, as far as your little power may admit, to the comfort and welfare of all your fellow-prisoners, and of those lately under your immediate command, especially.

We have a great number of prisoners in our possession, who are treated with the greatest humanity and kindness, and with pleasure I hear that Col. Arnold's detachment is treated in the same humane manner. The mischiefs of war are sufficiently great under the most civilized regulations. What a savage he must be, who would heighten them by unnecessary severity and rigor. I hope that humanity to the unfortunate will be the distinguishing characteristic of the successful on either side of this unhappy contest. Write to me often; and may infinite wisdom and goodness preserve and prosper my dear son.

Your very affectionate father,

SAMUEL WARD.

The son and his excellent guide and adviser never met again in this life—the latter dying of the small pox at Philadelphia, while attending Congress on the 26th of March following, and before the declaration of that independence for which he had so earnestly labored.

Captain Ward was exchanged in 1776, and on the first day of January, 1777, was commissioned as Major in Col. Christopher Greene's regiment of the Rhode Island line — a worthy compeer of his relative Gen. Greene, *Scipiados duo fulmina belli.*

In that capacity, he was present and coöperated in the gallant defence of the fort at Red Bank, when it was unsuccessfully assailed by the Hessians under Count Donop, October 22, 1777. The same year he was aide-de-camp to General Washington. The next year, he was detached for the defence of his native State, under the command of Generals Greene, Lafayette and Sullivan. In the celebrated retreat from Rhode Island, he commanded a regiment, and on the 12th of April, 1779, he was commissioned Lieut. Colonel of the 1st Rhode Island Regiment, to take rank from May 1st, 1778. During that and the following year he was in Washington's army, in New Jersey, and participated in the toil and glory of that service. He was present at the defence of the bridge at Springfield, by a part of the Rhode Island line, against the Hessian General Knyphausen, in June, 1780. He was an original member of the Society of Cincinnati, and through the war as the commander of a regiment was attended by his faithful body servant Cudjo, a full blooded African.

At the termination of the war, Colonel Ward returned to the peaceful pursuits of a citizen with the same alacrity that he had manifested when his country's voice had called him to arms. He now commenced business as a merchant, and manifested as much enterprise in his new profession as he had in his previous career. In the spring of 1783, he made a voyage from Providence to Canton, in the ship George Washington, which was among the first to display 'the republican flag' in the China seas. Upon his return to the United States, he established himself at New York, as a merchant, and by his probity, frugality and industry, became successful in his business. In the course of his mercantile career he visited Europe, and was at Paris when Louis XIV was beheaded. After his return from Europe, Col. Ward established himself on a farm at East Greenwich, R. I., where he lived to see his children educated to usefulness and establish themselves in the business of active life.

In 1816, with a view of being nearer his children, several of whom had embarked in business at New York, he removed from his native State to Jamaica, on Long Island. Here, and in the city of New York, he resided in the midst of his family and friends, by whom he was admired and beloved for his manifold virtues, until the termination of his long and useful career. His conversation, at all times interesting, was rendered peculiarly attractive to all who enjoyed an intimacy with him, by the discrimination with which he commented upon what he had seen and met with abroad. The politics and military operations of the Revolution shared also among the topics that were most agreeable to his mind; but rarely, if ever, did he allude to the actions in which himself had borne a part. The modesty which was so particularly striking in the military men of the Revolution made an essential part of his character. When death approached, it found him ready. A life nobly spent in the discharge of every public and private duty had prepared him to relinquish his Maker's gift without murmuring, and he descended to the grave,

> 'Like one who wraps the drapery of his couch
> About him, and lies down to pleasant dreams.'

Colonel Ward died in New York, August 16, 1832, in the 76th year of his age. In early life he married Phebe, daughter of Governor William Greene, of Rhode Island, thereby connecting himself by a double relationship with the eminent soldiers of that name. Mrs. Ward was born March 11th, 1760, and died October, 1828, in the 69th year of her age.* The issue of this marriage was

William Greene Ward, born April 1, 1779; died August, 1798.
Samuel, " 1780-1; died at the age of four or five years.
Henry, " 1782-3; " in infancy.
Henry,† " Mar. 17, 1784; " July 26, 1838.
Samuel,‡ " May 1, 1786; " Nov. 27, 1839.

---

*In the preparation of this biography, a sketch of Colonel Ward published in the American Annual Register for 1833, has been used entire; also a newspaper sketch written by the late Dr. John W. Francis, of New York. With these, particulars obtained from private and public sources have been incorporated.

†Henry Ward was the eldest surviving son of Captain Samuel Ward, and hence became a member of the Society of Cincinnati, succeeding his father. By the same rule of succession, Henry Hall Ward, Esq , only son of Henry and Eliza Hall Ward, and head of the Banking House of Ward & Company, New York, became a member of the Society of Cincinnati, and is at present its Treasurer. Mr. Ward is also President of the New York Club. He was for many years connected with the military of New York.

‡Samuel Ward was a partner in the old firm of Prime, Ward and King, New York.

Anne Catharine,	born	1788;	died Sept., 1837.
Phebe,	"	1790 or, 91;	" April, 1825.
Richard Ray,	"	Nov. 17, 1795.	
John,*	"	Oct. 26, 1797;	" March 31, 1866.
William Greene,	"	Aug. 7, 1802;	" July 22, 1848.

A taste for fine arts, literature and military science appears inherent in the family of Governor Ward. William Greene Ward, a grandson of Colonel Samuel, and son of William G., is Brigadier General of the First Brigade, First Division of the National Guard of the State of New York. He stands unrivalled in his knowledge of military affairs. He was Lieutenant Colonel of the Twelfth regiment National

*Mr. John Ward never married. Several years of his early life were passed in Rhode Island. He returned to New York, however, in 1818, and was for a time clerk in the office of Messrs. Nevins and Townsend, brokers and bankers. In 1819, he commenced business under the old Globe Insurance Company; and in 1824, established the House of John Ward & Company, which firm was afterwards, in 1847, changed to that of Ward & Company,—his brother, William G. Ward, having been one of the partners.

He continued an active member of the House until the first of March, 1865, when he retired from business with the reputation of a sagacious and successful banker, a man of irreproachable integrity and of great purity of character. Mr. Ward was for many years President of the New York Stock Exchange, and one of the earliest, though not an original member of that board. By a resolution of the board, he was (a short time before his decease) requested to sit for his portrait to A. H. Wanzler, which now graces the walls of the New York Stock Exchange.

Mr. Ward, besides his sterling qualities as a man of business, was highly esteemed for his cheerful and kind hearted disposition, his amiable manners and acts of generosity, which were the uniform expression of his frank and noble nature. He possessed in common with his late brothers (Henry, Samuel, and William G. Ward,) a cultivated and discriminating taste in the fine arts, and like them, not unfrequently proposed suggestive themes for painting or sculpture. The series of paintings entitled "Cole's Voyage of Life," were the result of such suggestions. Mr. Ward was also a sincere friend of Thomas Crawford, the sculptor, who married his niece, and Crawford's admirable bust of Washington, finished with his own hands, graces Mr. Ward's late residence in Bond street. He was a subscription member of the Clinton Hall Association; also a Life Member of the New York Historical Society, having contributed to its building fund, the publication fund, and other objects. He was fondly devoted to his accomplished nieces, (daughters of Samuel Ward) Mrs. Julia Ward Howe, the poetess, wife of Dr. Samuel G. Howe, of Boston, Mrs. Louisa Ward (Crawford) Terry, wife of the artist, now in Europe, and Mrs. Anne Ward Mailliard, of Bordentown, New Jersey. It is to Mr. Ward and the widow of Mr. Crawford (now Mrs. Terry) that the New York Historical Society is indebted for "the Crawford Marbles," which have been so generously deposited in its Library and Galleries of Art. His brother Samuel was the first President of the Bank of Commerce in New York,* the largest National banking institution in the United States, the present President being Charles H. Russell, Esq., also a "Son of Rhode Island." Mr. Charles Hall Ward, son of the late William G. Ward, possesses a fine library, and is an able financier in the house of Ward & Co.

The last of the brothers is the venerable Richard Ray Ward, who is not only highly esteemed as a lawyer of the old school, but also truly remarkable for his deep interest in historical studies and antiquarian researches, as well as for his recollections of distinguished contemporaries.

*The first Cashier was the late George Curtis, father of the graceful orator, poet, and accomplished author, GEORGE WILLIAM CURTIS.

Guard of the State of New York, at Washington in 1861. His was the first regiment to cross Long Bridge to invade Virginia, and had the advance for some time. He commanded the regiment at Harper's Ferry all summer in 1862, where they were finally taken prisoners by "Stonewall" Jackson. In 1863, Colonel Ward and his regiment were in Couch's Corps, Dana's Division, Yate's Brigade, in the Pennsylvania campaign, which ended in the Battle of Gettysburg. During the draft riots in New York, Colonel Greene with his regiment, at the request of Maj. General Charles W. Sanford, rendered efficient service in guarding the City Hall, until the danger was over. John Ward, jr., a younger brother, served as Captain in 1862 and 1863, in the Twelfth regiment, of which he is at present Colonel commanding.

Lieutenant CHRISTIAN FEBIGER, a native of Copenhagen, Denmark, had held a Subaltern's commission in the Danish service. He was Adjutant of Arnold's forces. He was a generous, sympathetic man, and Judge Henry speaks in the warmest terms of his conduct in the wilderness. He was taken prisoner in the attack upon Quebec, and with the other prisoners was kept in close confinement. He returned to Philadelphia in company with Mr. Henry, having sailed from Quebec in the Pearl frigate, Capt. M'Kenzie, August 10th, and reaching New York September 11. Subsequently he received commissions as Major and as Colonel. He led the 11th Virginia regiment at the assault on Stony Point. In 1791, he held the office of Treasurer of the State of Pennsylvania.

Lieutenant SYLVANUS SHAW, of Newport, R. I., was one of the officers recommended by Washington to the favorable consideration of the General Assembly of Rhode Island. After returning from his captivity at Quebec, he was commissioned Captain, and commanded a company under Colonel Christopher Greene, at Red Bank. He was killed in that battle, Oct. 12, 1777.

Lieutenant EDWARD SLOCUM, of Tiverton, R. I., was also among the officers recommended by Washington to the favor of the General Assembly of his native State. He was a Captain in the Rhode Island line from 1777 to 1779.

Lieutenant WILLIAM HUMPHREY, of Providence, R. I., taken prisoner at Quebec, was subsequently a Captain in the Rhode Island line to the close of the war.

Colonel JAMES LIVINGSTON was a native of New York. He had long resided in Canada, and actively sympathized with the Colonies at the beginning of the war. He commanded a battalion of Canadians, and in the assault upon Quebec was directed to make a false attack with a show of firing of the gate of St. John. Something occurred to prevent this movement, thereby failing to create a diversion favorable to Arnold's detachment. He commanded at King's Ferry at the time of Arnold's treason. He commanded at Verplanck's Point while the Vulture lay off in the stream, and sent to West Point for ammunition to enable him to annoy the vessel. On the evening of September 25th, (1780) he was called by Washington to his head-quarters at Robinson's House, for the purpose of eliciting such information in regard to Arnold as he might be able to give.

Lieutenant COLONEL ROGER ENOS was from Connecticut. His career in the Expedition through the wilderness has already been related. After retiring from the army, he removed to Vermont, and in 1781 was appointed a General and Commander of the Militia of the State, and became somewhat conspicuous in public affairs.

BENJAMIN DURFEE, a volunteer private in Capt. Topham's Company, was taken prisoner,—escaped in June, 1776, and came home;—was taken again on Rhode Island, which prevented his applying for the pay due to him. The General Assembly, at the June Session, 1782, ordered the payment of his claim of £24, 10s, "silver money," to be allowed.

Captain SAMUEL LOCKWOOD belonged to Greenwich, Conn. He did excellent service in capturing the fleet of Carleton, at Sorel, and was taken prisoner at the storming of Quebec. He was afterwards a Captain in Colonel Lamb's regiment of artillery.

EBENEZER ADAMS, of Rhode Island, was a volunteer with Arnold, and afterwards a Captain of Artillery. He was one of the originators of, and a Captain in the expedition under Colonel Barton to capture Prescott in 1777.

General Sir GUY CARLETON, Governor of Quebec, was born at Newry, County of Down, in Ireland, in 1722. He achieved an honorable military reputation, and in 1786 was created Lord Dorchester. He died in 1808, aged 86 years.

CALEB HASKELL, of Newburyport, Mass., was a private in this expedition. He was probably in Capt. Ward's company, as twenty men of a Newburyport company at Cambridge enlisted to serve under him.

GEORGE MERCHANT was a volunteer in Captain Morgan's company of riflemen, and a man who would at any time, give him fair play, have sold his life dearly. While the army was in position before Quebec, he was one day placed on picket, but in an unfortunate position. Stationed in a thicket, where, though he was out of sight of the enemy's garrison, he could see no one approach, a Sergeant of the British "Seventh," who, from the manner of the thing, must have been clever, accompanied by a few privates, slily creeping through the streets of the suburbs of St. John, and then under the cover of bushes, sprung upon the devoted Merchant before he had time to cock his rifle. Merchant was a tall and handsome Virginian. In a few days, he, hunting shirt and all, were sent to England, probably as a finished specimen of the *riflemen* of the Colonies. The government there very liberally sent him home in the following year. He was the first prisoner taken at Quebec. He was a brave and determined soldier, fitted for a subordinate station.—*Henry.*

Lieutenant WILLIAM HETH, 2d, of Frederick County, Va., was blind of one eye. He was a brave officer, was taken prisoner at Quebec, and subsequently was made a Colonel. As mentioned elsewhere, he kept a Journal of the Expedition to Canada, which was used by Marshall.

Sergeant THOMAS BOYD was, in 1779, Captain of a company of riflemen in the First Pennsylvania regiment. The same year he accompanied General Sullivan in his expedition against the Indians of the Six Nations, in western New York, was taken prisoner by the savages, tortured and put to death.

Sergeant CHARLES PORTERFIELD was a native of Frederick County, Virginia. He marched as a volunteer with Arnold through the wilderness. He showed great bravery in the attack upon Quebec, and was the first man to scale the walls. With his companions he was taken prisoner. After being exchanged, he raised a company at his own expense, and was commissioned in the Virginia line. In leading a regiment of which he was Lieut. Col. Commanding, he was killed in the battle of Camden.

MICHAEL SIMPSON was from Pennsylvania, and a volunteer with Arnold, in Smith's company. At the time of the assault upon Quebec, he was, by order of Arnold, in command as Lieutenant at the Isle of Orleans. Henry says, he was "one of the most spirited and active officers, always alert, always on duty." Many years after the war, he was made a General in the Pennsylvania Militia.

Dr. Thomas Gibson was a Sergeant in Captain Hendricks' company. He was taken prisoner at Quebec. Of the part he took in the plan of escape, related by Captain Thayer, page 33, Henry makes the following relation: "Money was obtained from charitable nuns who visited the prison, but obtained in a method remarkable rather for ingenuity than fairness or propriety; but it was thought that all artifices were allowable, especially as life was to be hazarded for liberty. Once a nun was seen approaching; when Doctor Gibson, who had studied physic at Cornish, and who afterwards died at Valley Forge, in the winter of 1788, a young man of ruddy cheeks and with a beautiful head of hair, was hurried into bed, to play the part of a sick man with a high fever. The nun being introduced, crossed herself and whispering an Ave Maria or Pater Noster, poured the contents of her purse, 24 coppers, into the hand of the patient. The money procured powder, and the manner of obtaining it occasioned some merriment to cheer the gloom of a prison."

Robert Cunningham, of Smith's company, was a strong, athletic man, about twenty-five years old. He was a wealthy freeholder of Lancaster County, Penn. In this campaign he imbibed the seeds of a disease that hurried him to an early grave.

Sergeant Joseph Ashton, of Captain Lamb's company, was placed in chief command of the organization of the prisoners who had planned an escape. Under his orders were Sergeant Boyd, Henry, McKay and others, to serve as Colonels, Majors, Captains, &c. After being exchanged, he was commissioned Major in Colonel Lamb's regiment of artillery.

Captain Colbourn commanded a company of artificers in the march through the wilderness.

Lieutenant Isaiah Wool remained in command of Capt. Lamb's company after his capture. He was afterwards commissioned Captain of Artillery.

Sergeant Henry Crone, of Captain Hendricks' company, was descended from a worthy and respectable family of York County, Penn. He was a droll dog, and much inclined to play.—*Henry.*

Captain Matthew Duncan, from Pennsylvania, a volunteer, was sent to reconnoitre, after the attack on Quebec, and was taken prisoner.

Lieutenant James Tisdale, of Medfield, Mass., was wounded at Quebec, a ball passing through the fleshy part of his shoulder. He served in the Massachusetts line during the war.

NOTE N.

A List of Men's names in Captain Simeon Thayer's Company, being Part of the Detachment under the Command of Col. Benedict Arnold on the Expedition for Canada, at Cambridge, Sept'r, 1775. Abstract of Pay due to Capt. Simeon Thayer's Company, from Sep'r 1, 1775, to Jan'y 1, 1776.

Officers and Privates' Names.	What Capacity.	Returned Back Sick.	Taken Prisoners at Quebec, Dec'r 31, 1775.	Not taken Prisoners.	Sup'r Cr. The m'nth Sep'r pay 1775, at Cambrg.	Names of Men Listed Jan'y 6, 1776, in Quebec.	The Officers and Men. M'nthly Pay, from Sep'r 1, 1775, to Jan'y 1, 1776, is 4 months.
Simeon Thayer	Captain		Dec'r 31, 1775		£6 0 0		@ 120 s. £24 0 0
Lemuel Bailey	1st Lieutenant				4 10 0		@ 90. 18 0 0
William Humphrey	2d do.		do. do.		4 10 0		@ 90. 18 0 0
Thos. Page	1st Sergeant		do. do.		2 8 0	Jan'y 6, 1776	@ 48. 9 12 0
Thos. Ellis	2d do.			Dec'r 31, 1775	2 8 0		@ 48. 9 12 0
Moses Bryant	3d do.			do. do.	2 8 0		@ 48. 9 12 0
Samuel Singleton	4th do.				2 8 0		@ 48. 9 12 0
Morris Cockran	1st Corporal			do. do.	2 4 0		@ 44. 8 16 0
James Hayden	2d do.		do. do.		2 4 0		@ 44. 8 16 0
Silas Wheeler	3d do.		do. do.		2 4 0		@ 44. 8 16 0
Thos Low	4th do.		do. do.		2 4 0		@ 44. 8 16 0
Isaac Hawes	Fifer	Oct'r 26, 1775			2 4 0		@ 44. 8 16 0
Wm. Clements	Private		do. do.		2 0 0	do. do.	@ 40. 8 0 0
Benoni Patten	do.	do. do.			2 0 0		@ 40. 8 0 0
Eleazer Thayer	do.	do. do.			2 0 0		@ 40. 8 0 0
John Thomson	do.			do. do.	2 0 0		@ 40. 8 0 0
John Latham	do.	do. do.			2 0 0		@ 40. 8 0 0
Stephen Mills	do.		do. do.		2 0 0		@ 40. 8 0 0
Jonathan Scott	do		do. do.		0 0		@ 40. 8 0 0
Elijah Fowler	do.		do. do.		2 0 0		@ 40. 8 0 0
Rich'd Congdon	do.			do. do.	2 0 0		@ 40. 8 0 0
Francis Filibut	do.			do. do.	2 0 0		@ 40. 8 0 0
John Barritt	do.			do. do.	2 0 0		@ 40. 8 0 0
Rob't Hill	do.	Sep'r 26, 1775			2 0 0		@ 40. 8 0 0
John Turner	do.			do. do.	2 0 0		@ 40. 8 0 0
Wm. Willis	do.			do. do.	2 0 0		@ 40. 8 0 0
James Barnes	do.			do. do.	2 0 0		@ 40. 8 0 0
Moses Hemmenwey	do.		do. do.		2 0 0	do. do.	@ 40. 8 0 0
Andrew Hinman	do.		do. do.		2 0 0		@ 40. 8 0 0
Nath'l Parker	do.			do. do.	2 0 0		@ 40. 8 0 0
James Welch	do.			do. do.	2 0 0		@ 40. 8 0 0
Daniel Devizer	do.		Killed in Battle.		2 0 0		@ 40. 8 0 0
Abel Ford	do.	Oct. 26, 1775			2 0 0		@ 40. 8 0 0
Sam'l Ingalls	do.		Dec'r 31, 1775		2 0 0		@ 40. 8 0 0
Thos. Garey	do.	do. do.			2 0 0		@ 40. 8 0 0
Alex'r Spencer	do.	do. do.			2 0 0		@ 40. 8 0 0
Jesse Jewell	do.		do. do.		2 0 0		@ 40. 8 0 0

					£	s	d			£	s	d
Sam'l Williams	do.	do. do.			2	0	0		@ 40.	8	0	0
Elijah Jones	do.	do. do.			2	0	0		@ 40.	8	0	0
James Stone	Entered Man-of-	war, June 22, '76	do. do.		2	0	0		@ 40.	8	0	0
George Leach	Private	Deserted	Paid the three	deserters one	2	0	0		@			
Nath'l Pease	do.	Sep'r 25,	month Pay	and Clothing	2	0	0					
Joseph Lewis	do.	1776.	at Cam-	bridge	2	0	0					
Charles Nutting	Entered a Fish-			Dec'r 31, 1775	2	0	0		@ 40.	8	0	0
Peter Field	erman Jan. 6, '76		do. do.		2	0	0		@ 40	8	0	0
James Monk	Private			do. do.	2	0	0		@ 40.	8	0	0
Silas Hooker	do.		do. do.		2	0	0		@ 40.	8	0	0
Benj'n Diman	do.			do. do.	2	0	0		@ 40.	8	0	0
Patrick Trayna	do.		Killed in battle		2	0	0		@ 40.	8	0	0
Thos. Whittemore	do.			do. do.	2	0	0		@ 40.	8	0	0
Wm. Googe	do.	Oct'r 25, 1775			2	0	0		@ 40.	8	0	0
Joseph Jewell	do.	Oct'r 25, do.			2	0	0		@ 40.	8	0	0
Patr'k Hamington	do.		Dec'r 31, 1775		2	0	0	Jan'y 6, 1776	@ 40.	8	0	0
Jeremiah Mosher	do.			do. do.	2	0	0		@ 40.	8	0	0
Davis Williams	do.		do. do.		2	0	0		@ 40.	8	0	0
Caleb Gordon	do.			do. do.	2	0	0		@ 40.	8	0	0
Jabez Dow	do.			do. do.	2	0	0		@ 40.	8	0	0
Benj'n West	Entered a Fish-	erman Jan. 6, '76	do. do.		2	0	0		@ 40.	8	0	0
Jacob Flarnder	Private	Oct'r 26, 1776			2	0	0		@ 40.	8	0	0
Stephen Bartlett	do.			do. do.	2	0	0		@ 40.	8	0	0
Sam'l Blasdale	do.			do. do.	2	0	0		@ 40.	8	0	0
Jacob Good	do.	do. do.			2	0	0		@ 40.	8	0	0
John Robinson	do.		do. do.		2	0	0	do. do.	@ 40.	8	0	0
Cornelius Higgarty	do.		do. do.		2	0	0	do. do.	@ 40.	8	0	0
Matthew Philips	do.			do. do.	2	0	0		@ 40.	8	0	0
Isaac Fillebrown	do.	do. do.			2	0	0		@ 40.	8	0	0
Jonathan Jacobs	do.		do. do.		2	0	0		@ 40.	8	0	0
Pasco Auston	do.			do. do.	2	0	0		@ 40.	8	0	0
Joseph Bosworth	do.	do. do.			2	0	0		@ 40.	8	0	0
John Smith	do.			do. do.	2	0	0		@ 40.	8	0	0
Edward Mulligan	do.			do.* do.	2	0	0		@ 40.	8	0	0
Edward Conner	do.		do. do.		2	0	0	do. do.	@ 40.	8	0	0
John Hotley	do.	Sep'r 20, 1776			2	0	0		@ 40.	8	0	0
Banester Waterman	Enter'd Man-of-	war, June 22, '76	do. do.		2	0	0		@ 40.	8	0	0
Joseph Plastow	Private	Oct'r 26, 1775			2	0	0		@ 40.	8	0	0
Wm. Dixson	do.		do. do.		2	0	0	do. do.	@ 40.	8	0	0
Moses Eady	do.	do. do.			2	0	0		@ 40.	8	0	0
John Collins	do.	do. do.			2	0	0		@ 40.	8	0	0
John Rankin. Return'd	Oct. 1, '76, from	King's troops	do. do.		2	0	0	do. do.	@ 40.	8	0	0
John Ryand	Private	Sep'r 20, 1775			2	0	0		@ 40.	8	0	0
John Carrel	do.			do. do.	2	0	0		@ 40.	8	0	0
Sam'l Griffith	do	do. do.			2	0	0		@ 40.	8	0	0
John Cambridge	In the room of	Manie O'Daniel		do. do.	2	0	0		@ 40.	8	0	0
Daniel Lawrence	In the room of	George Durant	do. do.		2	0	0		@ 40.	8	0	0

Note II. Page 28.

The following list of the killed, wounded and taken prisoners of the American troops at Quebec, on the 31st December, 1775, is copied from *Ware's Journal*, several times before quoted. The asterisks are suffixed in the original, though no signification is given.*

Officers taken prisoners.—Lt. Col. Greene, Major Meigs, Major Bigelow, Adj't Febezer,† Captain Matthew Duncan.

York forces killed.—General Montgomery, Capt. Jacob Cheeseman, Aide-de-camp McPherson. 1st. Battalion, 8 killed and one wounded; 3d Battalion, 2 killed.

Capt. John Lamb's Company. *Killed.*—Solomon Russell, Martin Clark.

Wounded.—Capt. Lamb, Bartho. Fisher, Thos. Oliver, Ely Gladhill, Barns Burns.

Prisoners.—Lt. Andrew Moody, Capt. Lockhart, vol.;‡ Joseph Ashton, Sergt.; Robt. Baird, Robt. Barwick, James Arvin, John Ashfield, Gasper Steyman, Moses Brackit, George Carpenter, Thomas Winter, Jacob Bennit, Joseph Spencer, Thomas Thorp, John Conet, Joseph Dean, Benj. Vandervert, John Martin, John Fisher.

Listed in the King's service.—James Patten, John Poalk, John Wilson, Thomas Deys, William Whitwell, Thos. Morrison, David Stone, John Kelley, John Johnston, John Lacox, Wm. McLien, John Ritters, Peter Fenton, Shelby Holland, Peter Nestle [Matross,] David Torrey.

Capt. Daniel Morgan's Company. *Killed.* — Lt. Humphrey, Wm. Rutlidge, Cornelius Norris, David Wilson, Peter Wolf, John Moore, Matthew Harbinson, Rich'd Colbert.

Wounded. — Benj. Cackley, Solomon Fitzpatrick, Daniel Anderson, Spencer George,* Daniel Durst, Hezekiah Phillips, Adam Hizkill, John McGuire, Jesse Wheeler.*

Prisoners.—Capt. Morgan; Lt. Wm. Heath, 2d, [Heth]; Lt. Bruin, 3d, [slightly wounded]; Wm. Fickhis, Sergt.; Charles Porterfield, Sergt.; John Donaldson, Sergt.; John Rogers, Corp.; Benj. Grabb, Corp.; John Burns, John Conner, Solomon Veal, Jacob Sperry, Adam Kurts, John Shoults, Charles Grim, Peter Locke, John Stephens, David Griffith, John Pearce, Benj. Roderick, Thomas Williams, Gasper de Hart,* Benj. McIntire, Jeremiah Gordon, Rowland Jacobs, Daniel Davis, John Brown, John Oram, John Maid, John Harbinson, Jedediah Phillips, Jacob Ware, Absalom Brown, Thomas Chapman, Charles Secrests, Jeremiah Riddle,* William Flood, William Greenway, Rob't Mitchell.

Listed in the King's service.—John Cockran, Curtis Bramingham, Timothy Feely, Edw. Seedes, Patrick Dooland, Christopher Dolton, Rob't Churchill.

Capt. William Hendrick's Company. *Killed.*—Capt. Hendrick, Dennis Kelley, John Campbell.

Wounded.—John Henderson, John Chesney, Abraham Swaggerty, Philip Baker.

Prisoners.—Lt. Francis Nichols, Thomas Gibson (Sergt.), Wm. M'Coy (Sergt.), John Chambers, Robt. Steele, John Blair, Rich'd M'Cloer, James Reed, John

---

*On the 4th January, 1776, Colonel Allan Maclean, of the 84th Regiment of "Royal Emigrants," visited the prisoners and took their names and places of nativity. Those of British birth were required to enlist in this regiment, under the threat of otherwise being sent to England and tried as traitors. Under this threat many enlisted, and some doing so improved favorable opportunities to desert. This list of killed, wounded and taken prisoners is evidently incomplete.

† This name is written Febiger, Nebegry, Frebeeer, Foboger, and Phebeger. The correct orthography is Febigir.

‡ Probably Capt. Samuel Lockwood, Greenwich, Conn. A sea-captain.

McLin, Henry McGown, Edward Roddin, Daniel North, Matthew Taylor, Daniel Graham, Tho. Anderson, George Morrison, John Ray, Wm. Kirkpatrick, Wm. Gammel, Henry Crone [Sergt.], Jacob Mason.

Listed in the King's service.—Henry Turpentine, Joseph Greer, Sergt., Barnabas McGuire, Matthew Cunning, Daniel Carlisle, Richard Lynch, Philip Maxwell, Peter Burns, Thomas Witherup, Thomas Murdock, Francis Furlow, Wm. Shannon, Edw'd Morton, Roger Casey, Wm Snell, George Morrow, Daniel M'Cleland, James Ireland, Daniel O'Hara, Michael Young, John Hardy, James Greer, Peter Frainer, James Hogge, William Burns, Wm. O'Hara, Alexander Burns, Joseph Caskey, John Cove, Arch'd McFarlin, Thomas Greer, William Smith, Joseph Wright, John Carswell, John Gardner, Thomas Liebe.

Capt. Smith's Company. *Killed.*—Alexander Elliot, Henry Miller, Ingrabart Mortworth, James Angles.

Wounded.—Lt. Rich'd Steele, John Miller, Thomas Silborne, Peter Carbough.

Prisoners.—Robt. Cunningham, Thomas Boyd, Sergt., Sam'l Carbough, Philip Newhouse, Conrad Meyers, Conrad Sheyers, Valentine Willey, John Shaeffer [drummer], Michael Shoaf, Anthony Lebant, John Henry, vol., Edw. Egnew, Patrick Campbell, Joseph Dockerty, Nicholas Nogle, Thomas Gunn.

Listed in King's service.—Joseph Snodgrass, Sergt.; Henry Herrigan, Corp.; Henry McAnally, Michael Fitzpatrick, Edward Cavener, Timothy Conner, William Randolph, Rob't Richmond, Alexander McCarter, John Anderson, Hugh Boyd, Thomas Walker, Joseph Higgins, Daniel Crane, Henry Taylor, Thomas Pugh.

Capt. Handchitt's Company. *Killed.*—Lt. Sam'l Cooper, Nath'l Goodrich, Wm. Goodrich, Peter Heady, Spencer Merwick, John Morriss, Theophilus Hide.

Wounded.—David Sage, [Sergt.]

Prisoners.—Capt. Oliver Handchitt; Lt. Abijah Savage; 1Benj. Catlin, Quart.; Peletiah Dewey, Sergt.; Gabriel Hodgkiss, 1st Sergt.; Gershom Wilcox, Sergt.; Roswell Ransom, Corp.; Jedediah Dewey, Corp.;* John Risden, Samuel Biggs, Samuel Bliss, Rich'd Brewer, Sam'l Burroughs, Nath'l Coleman, Stephen Fosbury,* Isaac George, 2Isaac Knapp, Edw'd Lawrence, Joel Loveman,* 3Elijah Marshall, Daniel Rice, 4David Sheldon, Ichabod Swaddle, Jonathan Taylor, Solomon Way,* Noah Whipple, Abner Stocking, Moses White, 5Simon Winter.

Listed in the King's service.—6John Basset, Drummer; Patrick Newgent.

Capt. Topham's Company. *Killed.*—Charles King, Caleb Hacker, Hugh Blackburn.

1Written *Chattin* by Thayer.

2Enlisted out of Capt. Caleb Trowbridge's Co. into Capt. Hanchet's Co., for the Canada Expedition, Sept. 5, 1776.

3Enlisted out of Major Roger Enos' Co., about the beginning of September, 1775, into Capt. Hanchet's Co., Col. Wyllys' Regt., Col. Arnold's detachment.

4Son of David Sheldon.

5Was a minor, and an apprentice of Joseph Forward. Was dead January 31, 1777.

6John Bazzlo, Drum Major, Conn. State Papers, III, p. 649.

The following names belonging to Capt. Hanchet's Company are added from the Connecticut State Papers, Rev. War, III, pp. 649-650:

Samuel Bemiss.

Elishma Brandekee.

Joseph Lewis; was a soldier in Capt. Hanchet's Co., and was not taken prisoner.

Aaron Bull; was fifer of Capt. Hanchet's Co. at Quebec.

Jas. Morris; was of Capt. Hanchet's Co. at Quebec, not taken prisoner.

Daniel Judd; a soldier in Capt. Hanchet's Co., went out in Capt. Trowbridge's Co. from New Haven.

James Knowles; was the Ensign in Capt. Hanchet's Co.

Wounded.—Joseph Kennyon, Baker Garlin.

Prisoners.—Capt. John Topham, Lt. Joseph Webb, Lt. Edw. Slocum, Matthew Cogshall, Sergt.; John Finch, Sergt.; Reuben Johnson, Sergt.; Stephen Tift, Philip Rollins, John Darling, Oliver Dunnel, Wm. Underwood, Wm. Thomas, Isaac Bentley, Charles Sherman, Benj. Irvin, Benj. Durfee, Wm. Pitman, Wm. Clark, John Bentley, Jeremiah Child,* Thomas Price, Samuel Geers, Anthony Salisbury.

Listed in the King's service.—Daniel Booth, Sergt.; Michael Clausey, John Linden, James Green, Patrick Kelley, Tobias Burke.

Capt. Thayer's Company. *Killed.*—Daniel Davidson, Patrick Tracy

Wounded.—John Rankins, David Williams,* Peter Field.

Prisoners.—Capt. Simeon Thayer, Lt. Humphreys, Silas Wheeler, Thomas Law [Low], James Hayden, James Stone, Silas Hooker,* Jonathan Jacobs, Stephen Mills, Daniel Lawrence, Elijah Fowler, Bannister Waterman, Jonathan Scott,* Cornelius Hagerty, Benj. West, Jesse Turrell, Samuel Ingolds, Andrew Henman.*

Listed in King's service.—Thomas Page, Sergt.; Moses Hemingway, John Robinson, William Dixon, Wm. Clements, Edw. Connor, Patrick Hanington.

Capt. Goodrich's Company. *Killed.*—Amos Bridge.

Wounded.—Noah Cluff, Nath'l Lord.

Prisoners.—Capt. Wm. Goodrich, Lt. John Cumpton, Ashley Goodrich, Sergt.; Augustus Drake, Sergt.; Festus Drake, Daniel Doyle, Jabez Chalker, Benj. Buckman, Samuel Buckman, Paul Doran, John Parrot, John Lee, David Pettes, Caleb Northrup, Roswell Ballard,* Roswell Foot, Oliver Avery, Elijah Alden, Benj. Pearce, Abner Day, John Taylor, Josiah Root, Rich'd Shackley.

Capt. Ward's Company. *Killed.*—Bishop Standley, Thomas Shepherd, John Stephen.

Wounded.—Eng'r James Tisdell, Nath'l Brown, Corp.; Jabez Brooks.

Prisoners.—Capt. Samuel Ward, Lt. John Clark, Lt. Sylvanus Shaw, Amos Boynton, Sergt.; John Sleeper, Corp.; Samuel Halbrooks,* John Goodhue, John Shackford, Moses Merrill, Nath'l Babson, Enoch Foote, Jacob True, Josiah George, Ebenezer Tolman, Thomas Gay, John Stickney, Elijah Dole, Elijah Hayden,* Jeremiah Greenman, Enos Chillis, Gilbert Caswell, John Gridley, Wm. Dorr, James Rust, Joseph Pool, Israel Barrit, Bartholomew Foster,* Joseph Ware, Thomas Fisher, Joseph Osburn.*

Listed in King's service.—Charles Harkins.

[John Hickey was a member of Captain Ward's company.]

Capt. Hubbard's Company. *Killed.*—Capt. Hubbard, Sergt. Weston.

Prisoners.—Lt. Sam'l Brown, Jonathan Ball, Sergt.; Minath Farmer, Sergt.;* Luther Fairbanks, Sergt.; Thomas Nichols, Oliver Smith, Simon Fobes, David Patch,* Thomas McIntire,* Benj. Phillips,* Timothy Rice* [mortally wounded and died in the hospital], Joseph White, Aaron Heath, Wm. Chamberlain, Anthony Jones, Russel Clark, Paul Clap, Joseph Parsons, Samuel Bates, Luke Nobles,* Joseph Burr, Oliver Edwards, George Mills.

Listed in King's service.—Charles McGoire, Morris Hayward, John Hall.

[Twelve men of Captain Hubbard's company were from Worcester, Mass.]

Capt. Dearborn's Company. *Prisoners.*—Capt. Henry Dearborn, Lt. Nath'l Hutchins, Lt. Amos Andrews, Lt. Joseph Thomas, John Flanders, Jona. Perkins, Caleb Edes, Jona. Fogge, Wm. Taylor, Wm. Preston, Eben'r Tuttle, Moses Kimball, Joseph Smith, James Melvin, James Beverley, Jonathan Smith, Samuel Sias, Thomas Holmes, Moses Folnsby, Charles Hilton, John Morgan, Enos Reynolds, Eliphas Reed, Robert Heath, Elkanor Danforth, Nath'l Martin, Jonathan Norris, John Dohbin, John McCalm, Charles Budget, Samuel Hewes, Aaron Serjant.

Total Killed, 35; Wounded, 33; Prisoners, 372; Total, 440.

York forces.—Killed, 13; Wounded, 1.

Total Killed, Wounded and Taken, 454.

MEMORANDA.

Captain —— AYRES led a body of pioneers through the wilderness to blaze trees and "snag" bushes, "so that he might proceed in perfect security."—*Henry*.

Lieutenant ANDREW MOODY, of Capt. Lamb's company, after being exchanged, received the commission of Captain.

Lieutenant WILLIAM CROSS "was a handsome little Irishman, always neatly dressed, and commanded [on the Isle of Orleans] a detachment of about twenty men." He was not in the attack on Quebec.—*Henry*.

Sergeant William McCoy, of Hendrick's company, was an excellent clerk, and came into favor with Governor Carleton by giving to Major Murray, of the garrison, a copy of his journal of the route through the wilderness into Canada. He was a sedate and sensible man.—*Henry*.

—— Metcalf, was a volunteer from Pennsylvania.

Peter Nestle, of Lamb's artillery, enlisted in the British service to secure an opportunity to escape, which he did, and joined the company at Montreal. He was made a subaltern.

John Tidd was a skillful boatman, and very useful in his vocation during the march through the wilderness.

John M. Taylor, "keen and bold as an Irish grey-hound," a ready penman and excellent accountant, was made by Colonel Arnold purveyor and commissary in the wilderness.—*Henry*.

William Reynolds, or Rannels, of Smith's company, "was miserably sick, and returned in the boats." Oct. 4, Mr. Henry purchased his rifle for twelve dollars. It was short, carried about forty-five balls to the pound, the stock greatly shattered, and worth not over forty shillings. Never did a gun, ill as its appearance was, shoot with greater certainty. Previous to this purchase, Henry had lost his hat, knapsack and rifle, in the river by the upsetting of his boat, as it swept down a rapid.

John Shaeffer was a drummer, and purblind. In the course of the toilsome march he would frequently, in crossing ravines on logs, tumble, drum and all, into the abyss below. This man, blind, starving, and almost naked, bore his drum (which was unharmed by all its jostlings) safely to Quebec, when many other hale men died in the wilderness. He was a brother of Jacob Shaeffer, a respectable citizen of Lancaster, Penn. Army life did not improve his habits.—*Henry*.

Jesse Wheeler was an excellent shot, and his rifle was in frequent requisition to procure game in the march through the wilderness.

Timothy Connor and Edward Cavanagh were Irishmen. Both settled in Pennsylvania after the war. The legislature of that State granted the latter a pension.

James Dougherty was employed as a boatman in the expedition through the wilderness.

J. M. Gwinn was a volunteer from Virginia.

John Martin, of Capt. Lamb's company, was a hardy, daring, and active young man. He undertook to convey to the American camp intelligence of the purpose of the prisoners to attempt an escape. In this hazardous enterprise he was successful.—*Henry*.

List of Balances due to Sundry Soldiers in the Year 1776.

Name	£	s.	d.
Luther Trowbridge	£4	4	4
Thomas Gould	3	7	7
Thomas Botter	3	0	6
John Baldarce		15	0
Jabez Brooks	3	4	7
Aaron Cleveland	5	9	10
John Chaplin	2	8	10
Joseph Fasset	3	17	4
Thomas Dougherty	2	0	5
Elijah Haden	2	3	4
Benjamin M. Kinney	3	6	8
Ebenezer Langley	3	12	1
John Carr Roberts	4	6	8
Enoch Richardson	5	8	2
Bishop Stanley	1	8	5
John Stevens	3	14	1
Thomas Smith	3	1	8
John Clarke	1	15	9
James Williams		10	8
	£52	18	11

I certify that Lieut. Colonel Samuel Ward, in the final settlement of his account with the United States, accounted for the sum of one hundred and ninety-two dollars and 44-100, as due to the individuals contained on the within List, and that sum was deducted out of his account as valued by the scale of depreciation on the first of January, 1778, a 4 for 1.

John White, Clerk.

Capt. Samuel Ward,

To Benedict Arnold.

Sept. 11, 1775. Bill Clothing furnished his Company at Cambridge, by the Qr. Mr. Gen'l, viz:

[Here follow the items.]

Towards the end money was charged to

26 Sept'r. Thomas Dougherty, Jabez Brooks, John Hickey, who were doubtless members of Capt. Ward's Company.

Note I. Page 33.

As some matches might be necessary in that event [viz: overcoming the guard at St. John's gate, and turning the cannon upon the city,] and there would be occasion for powder, in was procured in the following ingenious way. Some small gun carriages were made, mounted with paper cannon, a few inches in length. Embrasures were cut with a knife in the front board of the berths on opposite sides of the room; and two parties were formed for the pigmy contest. The blaze and report, as loud as small pistols, created much merriment. For this sport, many cartridges were obtained, most of which were carefully laid aside for other purposes.—*Henry.*

Note K.

Sedgwick, in his History of Sharon, (pp. 45, 46,) states that a company from that town marched under Montgomery to Canada, and that four members of that company were with Colonel Ethan Allen in his attempt on Montreal, viz: "Adonijah Maxam, David Goff, William Gray, and Samuel Lewis. They, together with Roger Moore, of Salisbury, were among those who were carried to England with Allen. Alexander Spencer, of Sharon, joined Arnold's expedition through the wilderness, but died on the march.

Note L.

The author of the History of Connecticut states that Morgan took command after Arnold received his wound and was taken to the hospital. This is an error. Arnold's division in the assault was a battalion organization, and his second in command was Lieut. Colonel Greene, and his third, Major Meigs. According to Dr. Senter's Journal, (p. 34,) after Arnold retired from the field, the division was "under the command of Lieut. Colonel Greene." Morgan joined Arnold with a single company of riflemen from Virginia, and was at no time in a position to rank Lieut. Colonel Greene.

Note M.

Letters from Colonel Arnold to General Washington.

Second Portage from Kennebec to the Dead River, Oct. 13, 1775.

May it please Your Excellency:

A person going down the river presents the first opportunity I have had of writing your Excellency since I left Fort Western; since which we have had a very fatiguing time. The men in general not understanding batteaux have been obliged to wade and haul them for more than half way up the river. The last division is just arrived except a few batteaux. Three divisions are over the first carrying place, and as the men are in spirits I make no doubt of reaching the Chaudiere river in eight or ten days; the greatest difficulty being, I hope, already past. We have now with us about twenty-five days' provisions for the whole detachment, consisting of about nine hundred and fifty effective men. I intended making an exact return, but must defer it until I come to Chaudiere. I have ordered the commissary to hire people acquainted with the river and forward on the provisions left behind (about 100 barrels) to the Great Carrying-place, to secure our retreat. The expense will be considerable, but when set in competition with the lives or liberty of so many brave men, I think it trifling, and if we succeed, the provisions will not be lost.

I have had no intelligence from Gen. Schuyler or Canada, and expect none until I reach Chaudiere pond, where I expect a return of my express and to determine my plan of operation; which, as it is to be governed by circumstances, I can say no more than if we are obliged to return, I believe we shall have a sufficiency of provisions to reach this place, where the supply ordered the commissary to send forward, will enable us to return on our way home so far, that your Excellency will be able to relieve us. If we proceed on we shall have sufficient stock to reach the French inhabitants, when we can be supplied, if not Quebec.

I am with the greatest respect,
Your Excellency's most obed't, h'ble serv't,
B. Arnold.

P. S. Your Excellency may possibly think we have been tardy in our march, as we have gained so little; but when you consider the badness and weight of the batteaux and the large quantity of provisions, &c., we have been obliged to force up against a very rapid stream, where you would have taken the men for amphibious animals, as they were great part of the time under water; add to this the great fatigue in portage, you will think I have pushed the men as fast as could possibly have been. The officers, volunteers and privates, have in general acted with the greatest spirit and industry.

Inclosed is a copy of my journal, which I fancied your Excellency might be glad to see.

Chaudiere Pond, 27th Oct., 1775.

May it please your Excellency:

My last, of the 13th inst. from Portage to the Dead River, advising your Excellency of our proceedings, I make no doubt you have received. I then expected to have reached this place by the 24th inst., but the excessive heavy rains and bad weather have much retarded our march. I have this minute arrived here with seventy men, and met a person on his return, whom I sent down some time since to the French inhabitants. He informs me they appear very friendly, and by the best information he could get, will very gladly join us. He says they informed him Gen. Schuyler had had a battle with the regular troops at or near St. John's, in which the latter lost in killed and wounded, near 500; (this account appears very imperfect) and that there were few or none of the king's troops at Quebec, and no advice of our coming.

Three days since, I left the principal part of the detachment about three leagues below the Great Carrying-place; and as our provisions were short, by reason of losing a number of loaded batteaux at the falls and rapid waters, I ordered all the sick and feeble to return, and wrote Cols. Enos and Greene to bring on in their divisions no more men than they could furnish with fifteen days' provisions, and to send back the remainder to the commissary. As the roads prove much worse than I expected, and the season may possibly be severe in a few days, I am determined to set out immediately with five batteaux and about fifteen men for Sartigan which I expect to reach in three or four days, in order to procure a supply of provisions and forward back to the detachment; the whole of which I don't expect will reach them in less than eight or ten days. If I find the enemy are not apprised of our coming, and there is any prospect of surprising the city, I shall attempt it as soon as I have a proper number of men up. If I should be disappointed in my prospect that way, I shall await the arrival of the whole and endeavor to cut off their communication with Gov. Carleton, who, I am told, is at Montreal.

Our march has been attended with an amazing deal of fatigue, which the officers and men have borne with cheerfulness. I have been much deceived in every account of our route, which is longer and has been attended with a thousand difficulties I never apprehended; but if crowned with success and conducive to the public good, I shall think it but trifling.

I am with the greatest respect,

Your Excellency's most obed't h'ble serv't,

B. Arnold.

P. S. As soon as I can get time, shall send your Excellency a continuation of my journal.

B. A.

Point Levi, Nov. 8, 1775.

May it please your Excellency;

My last letter was of the 27th of October, from Chandiere pond, advising your Excellency that as the detachment were short of provisions (by reason of losing many of our batteaux) I had ordered Col. Enos to send back the sick and feeble, and those of his division who could not be supplied with fifteen days' provisions, and that I intended proceeding the next day with fifteen men to Sartigan, to send back provisions to the detachment. I accordingly set out the 28th, early in the morning, descended the river, amazingly rapid and rocky, for about twenty miles, when we had the misfortune to stave three of the batteaux and lose their provisions, &c., but happily, no lives. I then divided the little provisions left, and proceeded on with the two remaining batteaux and six men, and very fortunately reached the French inhabitants the 30th at night, who received us in the most hospitable manner, and sent off early the next morning a supply of fresh provisions, flour, &c., to the detachment, who are all happily arrived (except one man drowned and one or two sick—and Col. Enos's division, who, I am surprised to hear, are all gone back,) and are here and within two or three days' march. I have this minute received a letter from Brig. Gen. Montgomery, advising of the reduction of Chambly, &c. I have had about forty savages join me and intend as soon as possible crossing the St. Lawrence.

I am just informed by a friend from Quebec that a frigate of 26 guns and two transports with 150 recruits, arrived there last Sunday, which with another small frigate and four other small armed vessels at the river, is all the force they have, except the inhabitants, very few of whom have taken up arms, and those by compulsion, who declare (except a few English) that they will lay them down when attacked. The town is very short of provisions, but well fortified. I shall endeavor to cut off their communication with the country, which I hope to be able to effect and bring them to terms, or at least keep them in close quarters until the arrival of Gen. Montgomery, which I wait with impatience. I hope, at any rate, to effect a junction with him at Montreal.

I am with the greatest respect,

Your Excellency's most obd. servt.,

B. Arnold.

FORT WILLIAM HENRY. Note Q, Page 71.*

The perilous situation of Fort William Henry was known in Rhode Island some days before its fall, and intense interest was everywhere excited. The day following that event, the General Assembly met at Newport and ordered that one-sixth part of the whole militia of the Colony be forthwith raised and sent to Albany to operate under the commander-in-chief of His Majesty's forces near Lake George for the preservation of the country from the ravages of the enemy. On the 11th of August, Capt. G. Christie, A. D. Q. M. G., wrote from Albany to Gov. Greene, announcing the capture of the Fort, and mentioning the barbarities that had been practised by the savage allies of the French upon the retiring and defenceless garrison. The feeling awakened in Providence by these tidings, found a strong and patriotic expression in the following paper, drawn up and signed by many prominent citizens, and now for the first time made public:

Whereas the British Colonies in America are invaded by a large Army of French and Indian Enemies, who, have already possessed themselves of Fort William Henry, and are now on their march to penetrate further into this Country; and from whom we have nothing to expect, should they succeed in their enterprize, but Death and Devastation: And, as his Majesties principal Officers in the parts Invaded, have in the most pressing and moveing manner, called on all his Majesties faithfull Subjects for Assistance to defend the Country Therefore, we whose Names are Underwritten, thinking it our Duty to do every thing in our power for the Defence of our Libertys, Familys, and Propertys, are Willing and agree to enter Voluntarily into the Service of our Country, and go in a Warlike manner against the Common Enemy, and hereby call upon and invite all our Neighbours who have Familys, and Propertys to Defend, to Join with us in this Undertaking, Promiceing to March as Soon as we are Two Hundred and Fifty in Number, recommending our Selves and our Cause to the Favourable Protection of Almighty God.

Providence, August 15th, 1757.

STEPHEN HOPKINS	NICHOLAS BROWN
OBADIAH BROWN	JOSEPH BROWN
NICHOLAS COOK	WILLIAM WHEATON
BARZILLAI RICHMOND	WILLIAM SMITH
JOSEPH BUCKLIN	JONATHAN CLARK
JOHN RANDALL	JONATHAN BALLOU
JOHN COLE	JAMES THURBER
GIDEON MANCHESTER	AMOS KINNICUTT
EPHRAIM BOWEN, Surgeon	NATHL. OLNEY
JOHN WATERMAN	JOSEPH LAWRENCE
JOSEPH ARNOLD	THEOPHILUS WILLIAMS
JOHN BASS, Chaplain	JOHN POWER
JOHN THOMAS, Junr.	BENJAMIN OLNEY
ALLEN BROWN	GEORGE HOPKINS
BENONI PEARCE	EDWARD SMITH
BARNARD EDDY	JOSEPH WINSOR
BENJAMIN DOUBLEDAY	JOSEPH COLE

* For the reasons assigned in notes O and P, this and succeeding pages of the Appendix are printed without folios.

APPENDIX.

CAPTAIN SIMEON THAYER. NOTE R, Page 71.

In the escape from Fort William Henry, Capt. Thayer, then a private, became *broken-winded*. The heat created by running, and the sudden check of perspiration, caused by swimming across a stream, developed a virulent humor, which troubled him many years. It disappeared soon after he reached Quebec with Arnold's Expedition, and never afterwards returned. To the older men this expedition was a fearful adventure, and it subsequently told fearfully upon their constitutions. Those who had the spring of youth could recover their former elasticity and recuperate, whereas the chances were adverse to the seniors.

Captain [General] Thayer was with others associated in the ownership of the township of Lyndon, Vt., a grant in which Hon. Jonathan Arnold, a leading physician of Providence, and a representative in Congress from Rhode Island, was largely interested. March 31, 1781, Capt. T. sold all his right in the said township to Dr. Arnold for "nine hundred and seventy continental dollars." The following is the inscription upon his grave stone:

"Here rests the Body of Simeon Thayer, who died Oct. 21, 1800, in the 63d year of his age; Warmly attached to his Country, he early engaged in the war, which led to her Independence; a Prisoner on the Plains of Abraham; wounded in the battle of Monmouth, he suffered with cheerfulness for the cause he had embraced: nor did his Patriotism transcend his intrepidity. In the defence of Mud Island, he became illustrious by the prudence of his measures and the coolness of his courage, which could only be the offspring of a head unclouded, when the shades of death were gathering around him and a heart unappalled by the vision of his terrors to consummate his military fame. He was distinguished by the approbation of Washington, who knew that Major Thayer was a soldier indeed in whom there was no fear, and as a proof of the esteem of his fellow citizens he was chosen General of the Militia as a testimony of filial reverence."

NOTE S, Page 21.

The fate of JAMES WARNER, among others, was lamentable. He was young, handsome in appearance, and not more than twenty-five years of age. He was athletic, and seemed to surpass in bodily strength. His wife was beautiful, though unpolished in manners. Nothing was heard of the couple after entering a swamp on the march, November 1st, until December, when Mrs. Jemima Warner appeared in the camp before Quebec bearing her husband's rifle, powder-horn and pouch. It appeared from her story that Warner, unable to proceed, sat down at the foot of a tree, determining to die there. His wife remained with him several days, urging him, in vain, to proceed. The provisions divided to him at the head of the Chaudiere were nearly consumed, and having exhausted her powers of persuasion to advance, without effect, she left with him what bread remained and a canteen of water, and as necessary to preserve her own life, pushed on for the American camp. Warner probably did not long survive. Thus perished an unfortunate man, at an age when the bodily powers are generally in their full perfection. On reaching the habitations of the Canadians, Mrs. Warner was kindly entertained, and appeared in camp fresh and rosy as ever. This incident is but one of many that occurred that illustrates the dangers and sufferings of the wilderness march.—*Henry.*

APPENDIX.

CAPTAIN SAMUEL WARD. NOTE T, Page 85.

Captain Ward's commission was issued by the Colonial Congress, and was signed by John Hancock, President. The following is a literal copy of the original still preserved among family papers :

IN CONGRESS.

The DELEGATES of the United Colonies of *New-Hampshire*, *Massachusetts-Bay Rhode-Island*, *Connecticut*, | *New-York*, *New-Jersey*, *Pennsylvania*, the Counties o *Newcastle*, *Kent*, and *Sussex* on *Delaware*, *Mary-land*, *Virginia*, *North Carolina* and *South Carolina*, to Samuel Ward, Junior, Esquire.

WE reposing especial trust and confidence in your patriotism, valour, conduct and fidelity, DO by | these presents constitute and appoint you to be Captain of a Company, in the 12th Regi- | ment, commanded by Col. Varnum, | in the army of the United Colonies, raised for the defence of American Liberty, and for repelling every | hostile invasion thereof. You are therefore carefully and diligently to discharge the duty of Captain | by doing and performing all manner of things thereunto belonging. And we do strictly | charge and require all officers and soldiers under your command, to be obedient to your orders, as | Captain. And you are to observe, and follow such orders and directions from | time to time as you shall receive from this or a future Congress of the United Colonies, or Committee of | Congress, for that purpose appointed, or Commander in Chief for the time being of the Army of the United | Colonies, or any other your superior officer, according to the rules and discipline of war, in pursuance of the | trust reposed in you.

This Commission to continue in force until revoked by this or a future Congress.

July 1st, 1775. *By Order of the Congress.*

JOHN HANCOCK, President.

Attest, CHAS. THOMSON, Secy.

The Superscription.

SAMUEL WARD, JR., Capt.

At Cambridge, Capt. Ward received marked attention from General Washington. It is said he was the first officer of his grade there invited to dine with the Commander in-Chief. In a letter from the General to Governor Samuel Ward, dated at Cambridge, August, 1775, he says : " I did not know till yesterday that you had a son in the army ; to-day I had the pleasure of his company at dinner together with General Greene ; Colonels Varnum and Hitchcock had already done me that favor. I think if occasion should offer, I shall be able to give you a good account of your son, as he seems a sensible well informed young man."

In October, 1775, Governor Cooke, accompanied by Hon. Henry Ward, Secretary of State of Rhode Island, went to Cambridge to meet a Committee of Congress, to talk over and arrange matters requisite for the benefit of the army. This committee, consisting of Dr. Franklin, Colonel Harris and Mr. Lynch, arrived Oct. 15. Concerning these gentlemen General Nathanael Greene writes as follows: " I had the honor to be introduced to that very great man, Dr. Franklin, whom I viewed with silent admiration during the whole evening. 'Attention watched his lips, and conviction closed his periods.' Colonel Harris is a very facetious, good humored, sensible, spirited gentleman ; he appears to be calculated for military employment. Mr. Lynch was much fatigued, and said but little, but appeared sensible to his inquiries and observations."*

* Johnson's Life of Gen. Greene, 1822, quarto, vol. 1, p. 39.

APPENDIX.

The following letter to Captain Ward, was written from Cambridge by his uncle, the Secretary. It came to light after the preceding pages had passed through the press, and is an exact copy of the original.

CAMBRIDGE, October 15th, 1775.

DEAR NEPHEW,

I last Night rec'd Letters from your Father who is well. I left Providence on Thursday & there saw Mr. Davids who was at your Father's House on Tuesday last. The Family with your Aunts (who have moved into your Father's House) were all well. Your Father informs me that the Congress have received such authentic Intelligence from G. Britain as convinces them that the Ministry are determined to make a vigorous Push for the Conquest of the Colonies, and the Congress are consequently determined upon the most resolute Measures.

The Army here is in high Health and Spirits. And nothing is wanted to enable them to drive the Enemy out of Boston but a sufficient Quantity of Powder. By the best Accounts I can collect, 3000 Men may be expected at Boston very soon; which is all the Force that will probably come this Fall. Should it please God to crown the Expedition you are upon with Success, I need not press you to use your Endeavours that the Army may behave with such Prudence as to conciliate the Affections of the Canadians. This is all the Paper I have which I will use in praying God to bless you, and assuring you that I am,

your affec'e Uncle,

HENRY WARD.

Capt. Ward.

The superscription to the above letter is as follows:

To

Capt. SAMUEL WARD,

In Col. Arnold's Army,

QUEBEC.

Favoured by Mr. Price.

The day subsequent to the date of the above letter, (Oct. 16) General Greene wrote from Prospect Hill, to Governor Ward: "I had the pleasure to hear from your son Samuel, the 26th of September. He was at Fort Weston, just going to set off on his journey. All in health and good spirits. I had the same apprehensions with regard to Samuel's health and strength to endure the fatigues of such a campaign as you had. I advised him to decline it; but the heat of youth and the thirst of glory surmounted every obstacle, and rendered reasoning vain and persuasion fruitless. Colonel Christopher Greene is gone with him. His going made me the more readily consent to your son's going. I gave the Colonel a particular charge to lend him a helping hand in every case of difficulty, and he promised that his aid should never be wanting. By several letters from Quebec, things wear a promising appearance there. If the expedition succeeds, and we get possession of Canada, we shall effectually shut the back door against them, and I make no doubt of keeping them from entering at the front. You may depend upon my influence to obtain Charles a commission in the new establishment."*

* Johnson's Life of Gen. Greene, 1822, quarto, vol. I., p. 39.

APPENDIX.

THE WARD FAMILY.—Note U.

The name of Ward or Warde, is of Norman origin, and found on the ancient Roll of Battle Abbey, England, as given by Duchesne, Hollinshed and Leland. Arms, as borne by the Family in America, and originally brought over from England.* Azure, a cross patonce or. Crest. A Wolf's head erased, proper, langued and dentated gules. *Motto.* Sub cruce salus.

John Ward, (1) who had been an officer in one of Cromwell's cavalry regiments, came to America, from Gloucester, England, after the accession of King Charles the II. He settled at Newport, R. I., where he d. in April, 1698, aged 79. His son Thomas, (2) who preceded his father to America, married 1. Mary ——?, by whom he had daughters, Mary, who m. Sion Arnold, son of Gov. Benedict Arnold, of Newport, R. I., and Margaret, who m. Capt. Robert Writington; m. 2. Amy Smith, (grand-daughter of Roger Williams,) and died September 25th, 1689, aged 48. He settled at Newport, about 1660, and Backus (History Baptists I, 516,) says 'that he was a Baptist before he came out of Cromwell's army, and a very useful man in the Colony of Rhode Island.' His widow (Amy) afterwards married Arnold Collins, and their son Henry Collins, (called by the late Dr. Benjamin Waterhouse, "the Lorenzo de Medicis of Rhode Island,") born March 25, 1699, died at Newport, R. I., about 1770. His eldest son Thomas, died December 22, 1695, in his 13th year. His second son

(Hon.) Richard, (3) born April 15th, 1689, married Mary, (daughter of John) Tillinghast, November 2, 1709; was many years Secretary, and afterwards Governor of the State in 1741–3, was present at the siege of Louisburg, 1758, and died August 21, 1763; his wife Mary, died October 19, 1767, in her 78th year. *Children:* Amy, born September 4th, and died Oct. 22, 1710; Thomas, b. October 21th, 1711, was for many years Secretary of the State, which office he held at the time of his death December 21, 1760, (for issue see Coll. R. I. Hist. Soc. iii, 310); Mary, b. December 10, 1713, m. Ebenezer Flagg, d. May 21, 1781; Elizabeth, b. Feb. 19, 1715, d. Aug. 27, 1717; Amy, b. July 21st, 1717, m. Samuel Vernon, of Newport, R. I. and d. January 17, 1792; Isabel, b. Sept. 19, 1719, m. Huxford Marchant, and d. February 5, 1808; Hannah, b. Sept. 24, 1721, d. Dec. 27, 1783, unmarried; John, b. Aug. 4, 1723, d. August 15, 1724; Samuel, (4) b. May 27, 1725; Mercy, b. June 3, 1727, d. Oct. 25, 1730; Margaret, b. April 14, 1729, m. Col. Samuel Freebody, of Newport, R. I., January, 1765, d. June 27, 1805; Richard, b. Jan. 22, 1730, d. Aug. 7, 1732; Henry, b. Dec. 27, 1732, m. Esther, (dau. Thomas) Freebody, of Newport, succeeded his brother Thomas as Secretary of State, which office he held, by successive annual re-elections until his death, November 25, 1797, at Providence, R. I., leaving one daughter Elizabeth, who m. Dr. Pardon Bowen, of that city; Elizabeth b. June 6, 1735, m. Rev. William Bliss, of Newport, and d. in 1815, without issue.

(Gov.) Samuel, (4) m. Anne (daughter of Simon) Ray, of Block Island, also a lineal descendant of Roger Williams, December 20, 1745. He died of small pox at Philadelphia, Penn., March 25, 1776. His tombstone at Newport, was erected by the State of Rhode Island. (For other particulars see note, p. 83.) His wife d. at Westerly, R. I., December 3, 1770, in the 43d year of her age. *Children:* Charles, b. 1747, was an officer in the Revolutionary Army, d. unmarried; Hannah, b. 1749, d. unmarried 1774; Anna, b. 1750, m. Ethan Clarke, and d. 1790; Catherine, b. October 2, 1752, m. Christopher Greene, (brother of Gen. Nathanael Greene) and left two daughters, and d. 1781; Mary, b. December 5, 1754, d.

*The Arms and Crest are still to be seen engraved on the monument of Gov. Richard Ward in Newport, R. I.

1872, unmarried; SAMUEL, (5) born November 17, 1756; Simon Ray, born October 4, 1760, was Lieutenant in Revolutionary Navy, m. Sarah Gardner, and died of yellow fever in West Indies, about 1790, leaving two daughters; Deborah, b. October 12, 1758, became the second wife of Christopher Greene, who had married her sister Catherine, and d. in 1805, at Potowomut, R. I.; John, born July 26, 1762, m. Elizabeth (daughter of Dr. Ephraim) Bowen, of Providence, and died at Brooklyn, N. Y., September, 1823, without issue; Richard, b. 1764, m. Eliza (daughter of Joseph) Brown, of Providence, where he died October, 1808, without issue; Elizabeth, born 1766, died at Warwick, R. I., 1783, unmarried.

(Col.) SAMUEL, (5) married March 20, 1778, to Phebe, daughter of Governor William and Catherine Ray Greene, of Rhode Island the latter a daughter of Simon Ray, and noted as the witty correspondent of Benjamin Franklin. For full account of Col. Samuel, see *ante* pp. 53–60, &c. He died in New York City August 16, 1832.† His wife born March 20, 1760, at Warwick, R. I., died October 11, 1838. *Children:*

William Greene, born April 1, 1779, at Warwick, R. I., died August 17, 1798, in New York, of yellow fever; Samuel, born January 23, 1780, died November 13, 1787; Henry, born September, 1782, died December 3, 1783; HENRY, (6) born March 17, 1784; SAMUEL, (7) born May 1, 1786; Anne Catherine, born August 19, 1788, died Sept. 14, 1837, unmarried; Phebe, born July 17, 1791, at Providence, R. I., died at Jamaica, L. I., April 22, 1825; RICHARD RAY, (8) born in New York, Nov. 17, 1795; John, born October 26, 1797, died March 31, 1866, in New York City. See biographical notice page 89; WILLIAM GREENE, (9) born August 7, 1802.

HENRY, (6) m. September 2, 1818, to Eliza Hall, daughter of Dr. Jonathan Hall, of Pomfret, Conn., and Bathsheba Mumford, of Newport, R. I., and grand-daughter of David Hall, D. D., of Sutton, Mass., and Elizabeth Prescott, of Concord, Mass., the latter a great grand-daughter of Rev. Peter Bulkley, famous in Cotton Mather's Magnalia. Mr. Henry Ward had a great talent for music. He was a member of the Society of Cincinnati in New York. See Note p. 88. He died in New York City, July 26, 1838. *Only Son:* HENRY HALL, born in the City of New York, senior partner of Messrs. Ward & Company, Bankers, at 54, Wall Street, New York; President of the New York Club; Treasurer of the New York State Society of Cincinnati; and senior Director of the National Fire Insurance Company of New York.

SAMUEL, (7) m. Julia Rush, daughter of Benjamin Cutler, of Jamaica Plains, Mass. (sister of the late Rev. Dr. Benjamin C. Cutler, of St. Ann's Church, Brooklyn, N. Y., and relative of Gen. Francis Marion, of Revolutionary fame,) in October, 1812. He had a fine gallery of Paintings in his residence corner of Bond street and Broadway, New York, (see *ante* pages 88 and 89,; also Memoir of Samuel Ward, by the late Charles King, in Rev. Dr. Griswold's Biographical Annual of 1841,) and died November 27, 1839. His wife died November 11, 1824. *Children:* *Samuel, formerly a banker, lately a diplomatist and poet; Henry, Jr. d. in New York, 1840, aged 22; Julia, died in infancy; Julia (wife of Dr. Samuel G.) Howe, now of Boston, Mass., and the talented authoress of "Passion Flowers," "Battle Hymn of the Republic," etc.; Francis Marion, a merchant, died in New Orleans, Sept. 1847, aged 27; Louisa W., m. 1. Thomas Crawford, the celebrated Sculptor; m. 2. Luther Terry, artist, of Rome, Italy; Anne W., (wife of Adolph) Mailliard, of Bordentown, N. J.

RICHARD RAY, (8) m. November 3, 1835, Gertrude Eliza (dau. of Edward) Doughty, of New York. She died May 21, 1839. He is a lawyer in New York. (See page 81.) *Children:* Gertrude Ray and Annie Catrena.

† In Col. Trumbull's painting of the Death of Montgomery at Quebec, the middle soldier of the three grouped in the left foreground, was Capt. Ward. The artist painted the picture in Europe, without having a portrait of Capt. W., the latter being at the time in America.

WILLIAM GREENE, (9) m. Abby Maria (dau. of Dr. Jonathan) Hall, of Pomfret, Conn., (and sister of the eminent lawyers David P. Hall, and the late Jonathan Prescott Hall,) November 17, 1830. He died in New York, July 22, 1848. (See page 83.) He was possessed of unusual business capacity, and noted for his excellent judgment of men and affairs. His energy was indomitable. Mrs. Abby Maria Ward, above named, was also sister of the late Miss Anne Hall, the artist, several of whose Miniatures rival those of Malbone and Isabey. *Children:*

- * William Greene, banker, and Brig. Genl. First Brigade, First Division National Guard of State, N. Y. (See *ante* pages 89 and 90.)
- * Charles Henry, banker and amateur artist.
- Anne Catherine, died in her 5th year, April 1840.
- John, died in infancy, January, 1838.
- John, graduated Doctor of Medicine at Union Medical College, is a lawyer, and Colonel of 12th Regt. National Guard, State N. Y.
- * Prescott Hall, lawyer, resides at present (October, 1867,) in Europe.

THE DEFENCE OF MUD ISLAND. NOTE V, Page 78.

"My design by this address is to rescue from seeming inattention, the brilliant conduct of Colonel, the late Major, Thayer, in the defence of Mud Island, in the river Delaware, from the 12th of November until the 16th of the same month, in the year 1777. To a person unacquainted with that transaction, all the glory would be ascribed to Col. Smith, of the Maryland line. He is a gentleman of superior talents, of fine sentiments, virtuous and brave! He commanded the garrison on Mud Island from the latter part of September, excepting a few days, till the 11th of November, when the command devolved upon Lieut. Col. Russell, of the Connecticut line. The fatigues and dangers of that command were extreme. Col. Smith supported them with uncommon patience and fortitude, but yielded to hard necessity. Lieut. Col. Russell, an amiable, sensible man, and an excellent officer exhausted by fatigue, and totally destitute of health, requested to be recalled. * * * Major Thayer presented himself as a volunteer. The offer was accepted with inexpressible satisfaction. * * * The subscriber was personally knowing to all the facts before related. * * Should any of these facts be disputed, he will publish an attested narrative, which will silence envy itself."—*Letter of Gen. James M. Varnum to Bennet Wheeler, Aug. 2 1786.*

"On the 11th [November] in the afternoon, Col. Smith received a wound in the arm, and left the fort. Lieut. Col. Russell, of Gen. Varnum's brigade succeeded him in the command. On the 13th, Major Thayer went over and relieved Col. Russell, and the remainder of Col. Smith's men, part having been relieved before, with a detachment from Colonels Durkey and Chandler's regiments of Gen. Varnum's brigade."—*Letter of Col. Israel Angell, Feb. 17th, 1778.*

"Congress not having learned that the commander of Mud Island had been changed, voted that an elegant sword be presented to Col. Greene, of the Red Bank Fort, and another to Col. Samuel Smith, the commander of the Island, for their brave conduct in the defence of their several posts. The swords were to be made in France, and a year or two elapsed before their arrival and presentation, when Col. Smith had the modesty to receive the one which was justly due to Major Thayer, and but for the mistake made by Congress in the name of the officer who earned it, he would have received it."—*Letter of John Howland, late President of the Rhode Island Historical Society.*

---

* Married.

APPENDIX.

NOTE W—Page xviii. Introduction.

On the 22d of November, 1775, in view of impending danger, Sir Guy Carlton issued a proclamation at Quebec, ordering persons refusing to enroll their names in the militia lists, or to take up arms for the preservation of the city, to leave the place within four days, together with their wives and children, but forbidding their carrying away any provisions and stores belonging to them. This proclamation was soon after travestied in verse as follows:

GOD SAVE THE KING.

Whereas I'm chas'd from place to place,
By rebels void of sense and grace;
Crown Point, Montreal, Chamblee,
By Arnold and Montgomery,
From GEORGE and PETER§ are set free,
In spite of *Indians*, *D—l* and me!
In arms, before our walls, they reckon
With bombs and shells to fall Quebec on,
To burn our *Saints* * and hang our *Bishop*,
And spoil all business done at *his* shop:
Whereas also (c—se on such Catho-
Lics as those, they stir my wrath so)
Some went, and some who did enlist,
And carry arms of late desist;
Of which vile *miscreants* † this city
Rid must be, let who will pity,
Within *four days*, or by *St. Louis!*
They'l find that what I now say true is;
Before they've counted o'er their *beads*,
Or paid the *Priest*, or said their *creeds*,
As *spies* or *rebels* up I'll string 'em
Till to their senses I can bring 'em;
Each one who wont swear he's a tory,
I *sw—r* shall go to *Purga*–tory.
There to reform *in limbo patrum*,
And those who blame me may go a'ter 'em.
Let those who go take wives and children,
And haste forthwith into the wilder-
Ness 'mong *savages*, God knows,
They'l find for *cheer* frost, ice and snows;
Leaving behind all their *provision*,
Which I long since have had my wish on;
And *George Alsop*, my Commissary
Shall take thereof true inventory.
Given at St. Louis Castle, in
Quebec, the *year* of GEORGE sixteen,
Of Britain, France and Ireland King,
(Of *Rome*) the faith's *defender* being,
And so forth—by me GUY CARLTON,
Kennell'd ‡ and toothless yet I snarl on.
Witness *Harry T. Cramahe*,
My catholic liege Secretary.
Thus ends our BULL, and ten to one on't
Some *Yankee* 'll get it, and make fun on't.

---

§ The Pope. * Images. † Unsound in faith. ‡ Alluding to Guy, the common name of a dog and his being driven, with his blood hounds, into the wall'd city of Quebec.

Nc

A List of men's names in Capt. SIMEON THAYER's C
Colonel BENEDICT ARNOLD, in the expedition for Canad

Men's Names.	What Capacity.	Whose Company.	Whose Regiment.	Casualties
Simeon Thayer,	Captain.	......	Hitchcock.	
Lemuel Bayley,	1st. Lieut.	Tew.	Church.	
William Humphrey,	2d. do.	Aldrich.	Hitchcock.	
Thomas Page,	1st. Serg't.	Thayer,	do.	
Thomas Ellis,	2d. do.	do.	do.	
Moses Bryant,	3d. do.	Field.	do.	
Samuel Singleton,	4th. do.	Kimball,	do.	
Morris Cockran,	1st. Corp'l.	do.	do.	
James Hayden,	2d. do.	Thayer.	do.	
Silas Wheeler,	3d. do.	Field,	do,	
Thomas Low,	4th. do.	Thayer	do,	
Isaac Hawes,	Fifer.	Gridley.	Gridley,	
William Clements,	Private.	Fletcher.	Little.	
Benoni Patten,	do.	Gray.	Brewer.	
Eleazar Thayer,	"	Thayer	Hitchcock.	
John Thompson	"	do.	do.	
John Latham,	"	Field.	do.	
Stephen Mills,	"	Stebbins.	Brewer.	
Jonathan Scott,	"	do.	do.	
Elijah Fowler,	"	Tew.	Church.	
Richard Conden,	"	Bradish.	Finney.	
Francis Fillebutt,	"	Butler.	Nixon.	
John Barrett,	"	do	do.	
Robert Hill,	"	Fletcher.	Little.	
John Turner,	"	Stebbins,	Brewer.	
William Willis,	"	Powell.	Woodbridge	
James Barns,	"	Gray.	Brewer.	
John Bridges,	"	C. Olney.	Hitchcock.	Dismissed.
Moses Hemenway,	"	Thayer.	do	
Andrew Hinman,	"	Sloan.	Patterson.	
Nathaniel Parker,	"	do.	do.	
James Welch,	"	Field.	Hitchcock,	
Joseph Lewis,	"	Harris.	Bond.	Deserted Sept. 1
Charles Nutting,	"	do.	do.	
Peter Field,	"	Gleason.	Nixon.	
James Monk,	"	Thayer.	Hitchcock.	
Silas Hooker,	"	do.	do.	
BenjaminDiman,	"	Cranston.	Whitcome.	
Patrick Tracy,	"	Perkins.	Little.	
Thomas Whittemore,	"	Williams.	Graton.	
William Gouge,	"	Thayer.	Hitchcock.	
Joseph Jewell,	"	Ballard.	Fry.	
Patrick Harrington,	"	Perkins.	Little.	
Jeremiah Mosher,	"	Williams.	Heath.	
Davis Williams,	"	do.	do.	
Caleb Gorden,	"	Ballard.	Fry.	

* After the printing of the Appendix and Index had been completed, th
here inserted unpaged. The names are the same as found on pages 94 and
panies and regiments they were enlisted.

ompany, being part of the detachment under the command of
a. Cambridge, September 10, 1775.*

	Men's Names.	What Capacity.	Whose Company.	Whose Regiment.	Casualties.
	Jabez Dow,	Private.	Ballard.	Fry.	
	Benjamin West,	do.	Williams.	Heath.	
	Jacob Flander,	"	Ballard.	Fry.	
	Stephen Bartlett,	"	do.	do.	
	Samuel Blasdell,	"	do.	do.	
	John Blackford,	"	Hall.	Bond.	Dis'd in Cambridge.
	Abijah Adams,	"	Dexter	Woodbridge	Do. do.
	Jacob Good,	"	Thayer	Hitchcock.	
	John Robinson,	"	do.	do.	
	Cornelius Higgarty,	"	Field.	do.	
	Matthew Philip,	"	Hill.	Shermond.	
	Isaac Fillebrown,	"	Lock.	Bond.	
	Abraham Jones,	"	Kimball.	Hitchcock.	Dis'd in Cambridge.
	Jonathan Jacobs,	"	Wilder.	Little.	
	Pasco Austin,	"	J. Olney.	Hitchcock.	
	Joseph Bosworth,	"	do.	do.	
	Manie O'Daniel,	"	Field.	do.	Dis'd in Cambridge.
	John Smith,	"	Powell.	Whitcome.	
	Daniel Devizor,	"	Thayer.	do.	
	Abel Ford,	"	Kimball.	do.	
	Samuel Ingalls,	"	Hall.	Bond.	
	Thomas Geary,	"	do.	do.	
	Alexander Spencer,	"	Sloan.	Patterson.	
	Jesse Jewell,	"	do.	do.	
	Samuel Williams,	"	Brown.	Bond.	
	Elijah Jones,	"	J. Olney	Hitchcock.	
	James Stone,	"	do.	do.	
	George Leach,	"	Cranston.	Whitcome.	Deserted.
	Nathaniel Peas,	"	do.	do.	Deserted.
	John Salisbury,	"	Brown.	Bond.	Dis'd in Cambridge.
	Edward Mulligan,	"	Gleason.	Nixon.	
	Eden Conner,	"	Butler.	do.	
3th.	John Holley,	"	Talbott.	Hitchcock.	
	George Durant,	"	Whiting.	Brewer.	Dis'd in Cambridge.
	Banister Waterman,	"	Curtis.	Larned.	
	Joseph Plaistow,	"	Hill.	Shermond.	
	William Dixon,	"	Brown.	Bond.	
	Moses Eady,	"	do.	do.	
	John Collins,	"	McInster	Patterson.	
	John Rankin,	"	Elliot.	Putnam.	
	John Ryand,	"	Gleason.	Nixon.	
	John Canell,	"	Butler	do.	
	Samuel Griffith,	"	Dexter.	Woodbridge	
	John Cambridge,	"	Thayer.	Hitchcock.	In room of Manie O'Daniel.
	David Lawrence,	"	C. Olney.	do.	In room of George Durant.

* above list of Captain Thayer's company was placed in the hands of the writer, and is
5, but with the addition of the names of the Captains and Colonels, from whose com-

INDEX.

www.ingramcontent.com/pod-product-compliance
Lightning Source LLC
Chambersburg PA
CBHW030319170426
43202CB00009B/1065

* 9 7 8 3 7 4 3 3 3 2 4 3 0 *